Ferrier's

Judgment of Nativities

with an

Introduction

by

Christopher Warnock

2009

ISBN 978-0-557-20260-7

Renaissance Astrology Press
www.renaissanceastrology.com

 Renaissance Astrology

Renaissance Natal Astrology

Natal astrology is one of the four branches of traditional European astrology. Natal astrology looks at the horoscope at the time of birth of a person and uses that to foretell their future. Horary astrology looks at the chart of a question to answer that question. Electional astrology looks at the chart of an event to choose the most astrologically auspicious time for that event. Mundane astrology looks at a wide variety of charts including solar revolutions and eclipses to foretell broad events like weather, and the future of dynasties, countries and regions.

Astrology began in Babylonia and Chaldea and the first natal horoscopes date from around 400 B.C. Astrology diffused into the Hellenistic and Roman civilizations in the classical period and then reached the advanced Islamic civilization of the Middle East around 800 A.D. There Hellenistic astrology mixed with Persian astrology and the Vedic astrology of India. Astrologers, often Jewish, Persian or Christian, but working in Arabic, created a new and complex form of astrology. This Arabic astrology is the basis of traditional European astrology. Beginning in the 12th century A.D. Arabic astrology was translated into Latin and became available to European scholars.

One of the most influential medieval astrologers was Guido Bonatti, who wrote the *Book of Astronomy*, an encyclopedic guide to horary, electional, mundane and natal astrology. Bonatti's work exerted a tremendous influence on medieval and Renaissance astrologers.

By the 16th and 17th centuries the complexities of Arabic astrology had begun to be lost. Renaissance astrologers also began to believe that the Arabic astrology had departed from the pure "Ptolemaic" astrology of the Greeks and started to look upon its nuances with suspicion. In addition the spiritually based philosophy of the Middle Ages began to give way to the atheistic/materialistic philosophy of the "Enlightenment" which also had a negative effect on astrological theory and practice since astrology is at root, a spiritual science.

With the relaxation of censorship and other social controls during the English Civil of the mid-1640s and 1650s there was a great resurgence of interest in astrology and a large number of astrological texts were published. A Renaissance style of natal astrology, less nuanced than the medieval method epitomized by Guido Bonatti, became popular. One of the proponents of this style was the famous English horary astrologer William Lilly, whose *Christian Astrology* Book Three contains a complete exposition of Renaissance natal astrology.

Another popular Renaissance work on natal astrology was Auger Ferrier's *Jugements Astronomiques sur les Nativites*, published in Lyon in 1582. Ferrier was a well known physician and astrologer of Toulouse and wrote a number of books including a treatise on critical days "according to Pythagorean doctrine and astronomical observation" (Thorndike VI, p.479) as well as a work on dream interpretation. Ferrier was personal physician and astrologer to Queen Catherine de' Medici of France and a colleague of the famous Nostradamus. Catherine de' Medici was fascinated with astrology and magic and *Jugements Astronomiques* was dedicated to her. Ferrier's book was translated into English in 1593 by Thomas Kelway as *A Learned Astronomical Discourse, of the Judgment of Nativities*.

When we compare Ferrier's and other Renaissance astrologers' methods to those of the medieval astrologer Guido Bonatti we find a greater focus on house rulers and on the natural planetary rulerships. While in Arabic and medieval European astrology we also see the use of almutens, particularly over a large variety of points, multiple triplicity rulers and other specialized techniques, Renaissance astrology is clearly less complex.

Nevertheless Ferrier's *Judgment of Nativities* provides an excellent example of Renaissance natal technique which is still capable of accurate natal prediction and has the virtue of being much easier to learn than Bonatti's medieval natal methods.

Christopher Warnock

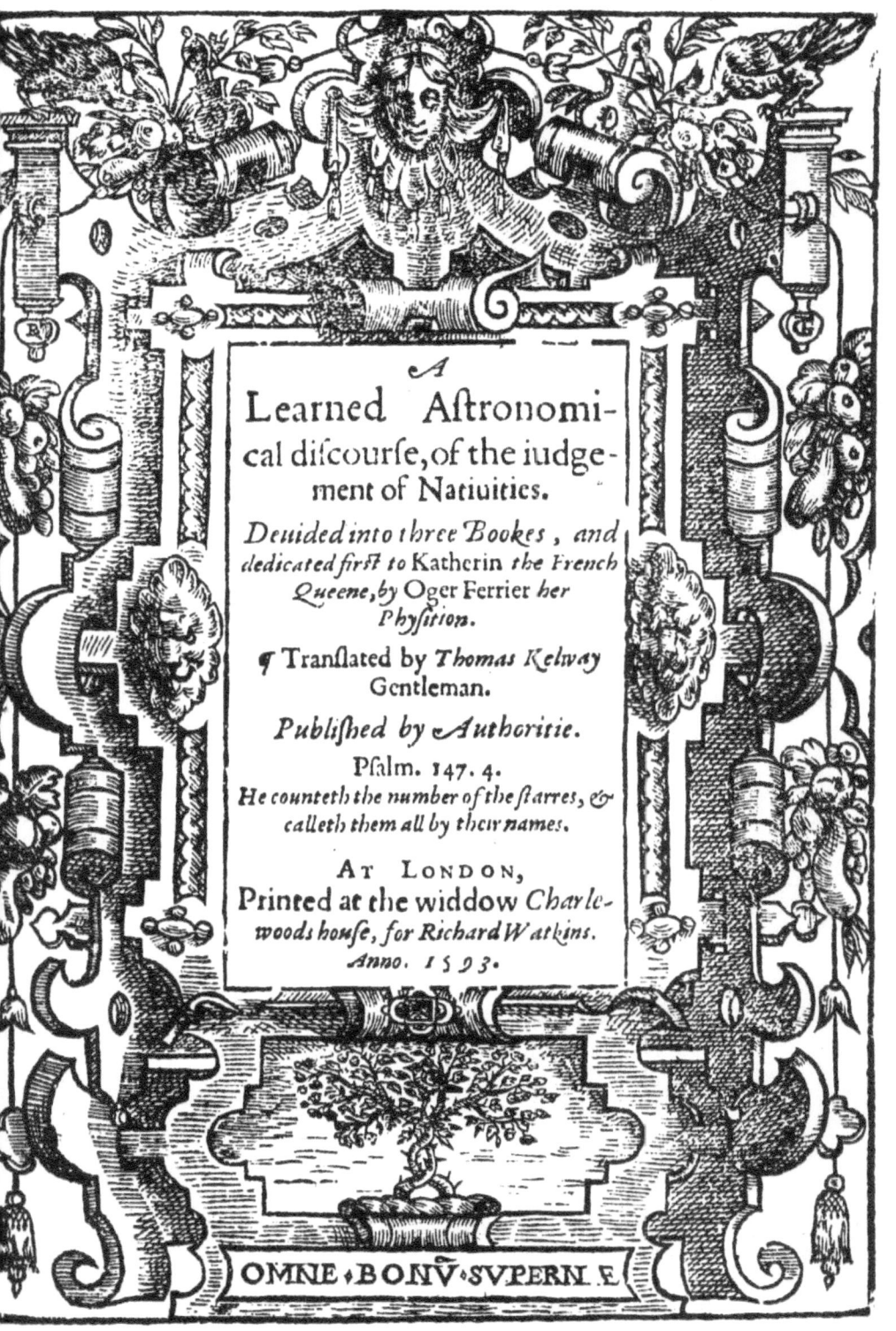

A
Learned Aſtronomi-
cal diſcourſe, of the iudgement of Natiuities.

*Deuided into three Bookes , and
dedicated firſt to* Katherin *the French
Queene, by* Oger Ferrier *her
Phyſition.*

¶ Tranſlated by *Thomas Kelway*
Gentleman.

Publiſhed by Authoritie.

Pſalm. 147. 4.
*He counteth the number of the ſtarres, &
calleth them all by their names.*

At London,
Printed at the widdow *Charle-
woods houſe, for Richard Watkins.*
Anno. 1593.

OMNE ⟡ BONV ⟡ SVPERNE

TO THE RIGHT HO-

NOVRABLE, VERTVOVS,
AND LEARNED LORD *HENRY*,
Earle of Northumberland:
(✱)

Lorde Percie, Lucie, Brian, Fitzpaine and Poynings: Lord of the Honors of Cockermouth and Petworth. &c. Knight of the moſt honorable order of the GARTER. All true felicitie both in thys life and in the worlde to come moſt hartily wiſhed.

IF that ſaying of *Plato* (right noble Lorde) be true, that our Countrey challengeth an eſpeciall intereſt in our very vttermoſt abilitie, which any way may tend to profit & benefite the ſame: then will it ſufficiently countenaunce the poore recciued Talent of myne, in that being ſo ſtrictly charged by ſo great and graue a Phyloſopher, I ought not to burie in obliuion my knowledge whatſoeuer, but rather as freely beſtow mine endeuour on her, as ſhee did franckly impart the light thereof to me.

For though it be a common phraſe in the mouthes of men altogether ignorant in the precious value and profite of Sciences : *That the ſtudie of Letters is a bottomleſſe Gulfe, and ſo long and ſo vneaſie a iourney, that they which raſhly thinke to finiſh it, oftentimes are drowned in the midway, and ſo vnder this pretence, account it better not to know much, yea, nothing at all :* Againſt ſuch ſlothful ſuggeſters of men in a deadly obſcuritie while they lyue, let mee auouch that ſaying of *Ariſtotle*, *Man* (ſayth he) *was created to vnderſtande and to doe, for knowledge begetteth iudgement, and by iudgement men execute all good and vertuous actions.*

O Science (ſayth *Plato*) *howe would men loue thee, if they did but knowe thee? for euen as health is the conſeruation of the body, ſo is knowledge the ſure and onely ſafe-garder of the ſoule.* And *Cicero* beeing of the ſame opinion, ſayth : *O knowledge, the guide of our life, the onely cauſe of vertue, and enemie to vice : What is the life of man without thee?*

If then (right learned Lord) ſuch a maine & current ſtreame of vnconquerable reaſon, waſheth to nothing the emptie and confuſed wits, of ſuch as are enemies to the excellencie of Arte, and maketh moſt fertile (like the ouer-flowings of Nylus) the iudgements of the that are gouerned thereby : (though farre from me be the thought of arrogating the very leaſt tytle of Arte to my ſelfe, yet as one that de-

ſires

THE EPISTLE.

fires to receiue the breath of life from her sacred dwelling, and holdes with the learned in all ages, that man is as a bruite beast without her:) then let me thus farre presume vnder your noble fauour, to shewe that I haue not altogether trewanted in my life time, but howe I haue bestowed those permitted howers of exercise, that more waighty affaires in the world affoorded me, both to declare my reuerende zeale to so high a misterie, and vnfeyned affection, I beare to your honor.

The worke was first written in French, by an excellent Scholler, *Oger Ferrier*, a Physition, borne in Tolouze, & dedicated to *Queene Katherine* of Fraunce, mother to the King that last deceaffed. And beeing now by me changed into an English habite, that it might receiue no indignitie by dedication, I haue stampt your noble name in the fore-head thereof, that it may bee sayde (in defpight of the proudest carper or controller,) Thys is the God-chylde of a peerelesse Godfather.

And as I doubt not of your honourable acceptauce, so I am likewise perswaded, that what hath wanted on my behalfe in tranflation, or any other imperfection beside, shall be as nobly censured: in which resolution I humbly kisse your hand, and continue as forward in affection, as any to your Honours welfare.

Thomas Kelway.

One of her Highnesse Trumpets in ordinarie.

TO THE COVRTEVS
Reader.

I Am to requeſt (gentle Reader) one fauour at thy hande, that if this worke of the iudgement of Natiuities ſeeme harſh and vnpleaſant to thee, thou wouldeſt not therefore wound the ſame with iniurious words, to charge thy ſelfe with more follie then needes : but if thou finde it aboue thy knowledge or capacitie, ſaie as honeſt minded Chion ſaid: Let my betters iudge of theſe matters. For I muſt and do confeſſe, that it is not a Booke for euerie mans reading , and hee that reades with deriſion, becauſe he vnderſtands not , muſt blame his owne inſufficiencie, and not the booke : for if hee could-learne as much in an hower, as coſt a learned man many yeeres to compaſſe, then would his humor be pleaſed , and the worke not reproched. But let ſuch loyterers vnderſtand, that knowledge requires the whole circuit of a mans life, and liue he neuer ſo long, yet may he learne : but if it might be attained in a Sommers daie, a number would be excellent , that through default thereof remaineth vtterly ignorant.

To vſe many words, I account needleſſe, knowing that the reproofe of the vnlearned, is rather the badge of their owne weake braine, then any blemiſh to a worke of worth : Therefore let them cenſure as they pleaſe, the learned (I know) will iudge like themſelues, of whom I had rather be deſeruedly controlled, then by the other be ignorantly commended.

Thomas Kelway.

The

✒ The Table of the matters in this prefent Treatife.

The firſt Booke.

The Table.

The ſecond Booke.

The third Booke.

Of

The Table.

FINIS.

OF THE IVDGE-
MENTS ASTRONOMICALL
VPON NATIVITIES.
The firſt Booke.

Chap. I.
Of the Celeſtiall figure of a Natiuitie.

FOR to iudge of Aſcendants and
Natiuities, after the traditions of the
auncient and learned Aſtrologians, it is
conuenient firſt to explaine the Celeſtiall figure, and in the ſame, to applie the
ſeauen Planets, with the head and tayle
of the Dragon *Lunaire*, together with the part of Fortune, and the part of the ſpirite and others, more appertaining to the high & notable ſignifications of the ſtarres;
Then, to ſette downe plainly the Celeſtiall figure, you
muſt in the firſt place, note the yere, the day, & the houre,
with the moſt neereſt minute of time of the natiuitie that
you haue vndertaken. The number of the howers and
mynutes, you muſt ſette them downe after the manner of
the numbring of the Aſtrologians, within theyr tables:
alwaies ſette downe the howers after-noone, as well by
day as by night, and neuer ſay, one hower, two howers,
three howers after midnight, but number xiij. hovvers,
xiiij. howers, xv. after noone. This done, ſearch in the
Ephemerides in the table of the yeere of your natiuitie, in
the right month & day propoſed, the degree of the ſigne

A.   wherein

wherein the Sunne is : looke afterwarde in the Table of houſes, which ſerue for the latitude of your Country, and ſearch there the ſaid degree of the Sunne vnder the lyne of the tenth houſe. And hauing founde in the ſame place the ſame degree of the Sunne, you ſhall find directly vpon the left hand of the ſame Table, a number of howers and minutes, the which write apart. To which number, you muſt adde the howers and mynutes that hath beene giuen you of the ſame natiuity, and that which reſteth by your addition, you muſt ſeeke in the table of houſes : and there where you find the ſame number of howers & mynutes comming of the ſame addition, you muſt take to a right lyne the poynts and beginnings of the ſixe houſes, which you ſhall finde marked : the which you ſhall direct vpon your figure, beginning at the poynt of the tenth, and continuing towards the left hand.

The beginning of the other ſixe houſes , you muſt take the oppoſite ſignes ; and if it happen that the number of houſes and mynutes, come to more then twentie-foure howers, it is then conuenient to ſubſtract twentie-foure howers of the ſame tyme, and the reſidue ſeeke out as we haue aforeſaid. If the hower of the ſame natiuitie, be vpon the poynt of twelue howers of noone, you muſt take the houſes in a right line of the degree of the ſunne, in the table of your latitude, without making any other addition, or ſubſtraction, and that when in the figure eſtimatiue : within the which, it is needfull by all meanes to apply the moouing of the Moone exactly calculated, according to the vulgare cannons of the Ephemerides, for to verifie afterwarde your natiuitie by the hower of the conception. As followeth.

CHAP: II.

Of the verification of the bower of the natiuity.

Leauing the Animodar of *Ptolome* and the meetings of *Schoner*, and all other vncertaine waies (although they haue theyr Authors) to verifie the howers of
natiuities,

natiuities, I will prefently follow the method of *Hermes*, approoued by long experience, and confirmed by *Ptolome* in his Centiloque, and by *Abraham Auenesrus* , by *Alphonce Leopolde, Haly*, and other moſt expert Aſtrologians. *Hermes* ſaith, that the aſcendant of a natiuitie, hath beene the place of the Moone at the tyme of the cōception ; and that the aſcendant of the conception, is the place of the Moone at the hower of the natiuitie. Who would be moore neere certified of the hower & mynute of a natiuitie, and of the true aſcendant, it is conuenient that you follow the doƈtrine of *Hermes* by the method folowing. Firſt of all that you looke into the figure eſtimatiue, whether the Moone be aboue the Horrizon or beneath. If ſhe be aboue the Horrizon, count the diſtance that is betweene the poynt of the ſeauenth houſe and the Moone : if ſhe be beneath the Horrizon , count the diſtance which is from the firſt houſe vnto the Moone, which diſtance of ſignes and degrees, you muſt ſearch in the table that followeth, vnder the title of the Moone, aboue the Horrizon or beneath, as truely you haue found in the ſaid figure. In a right lyne of the ſaid diſtance, you ſhall find the time that the infant hath remained within the wombe of his Mother, in a certaine number of dayes, the which you muſt reckon from the day of your natiuitie backward ; and there where the number endeth, you muſt marke the day of the conception, if the Moone be found in the ſigne of the aſcendant eſtimatiue. If you find her not in the ſame place, goe backwarde or forward certaine dayes of your account , vntill you haue founde the Moone within the ſaid ſigne, not farre from the degree aſcendant in the ſaid figure. The day conſidered , and in what hower, goe forwarde to the Eaſt poynt , the place where you haue founde the Moone in the figure eſtimatiue, and at that hower you muſt calculate the mæouing of the Moone. For this degree and mynute in the which you found her, you muſt place it in the aſcendant of your natiuitie.

A 2

And

And to know the hower in the which the place of the Moone of the natiuity, roſe to the Eaſt poynt at the time of the conception, take firſt the ouerthwart aſcention of the ſaid place of the Moone, within the table of the directions of your country, in the booke of *Iohn de Regiomonte*, of the ſame aſcention take away 90. degrees, (& ad to the whole circle which is of 360. degrees, when the ſubſtraction cannot be otherwiſe made) the reſidue ſhall be the right aſcention of the height of the poynt of the Merydian circle : take afterward the right aſcention of the Sun, and take out by the ſubſtraction of the right aſcention of the ſayd poynt of the Merydian, and adde 360. degrees if it be neceſſary, & turne that which is left into howers and minutes, in gyuing to 30. degrees two howers, to fifteene degrees one hower, to one degree 4. minutes of an houre, to fifteene minutes one minute of an hower ; by thys meanes you ſhall exactly come to the hower of the conception, to the which you muſt calculate the place of the Moone, and the ſame well calculated, put it to the poynt of the firſt houſe, in the figure of the natiuitie.

Diuers for this verefication doe dreſſe and garniſh the motions of the Planets foure figures. One of that hower eſtimatiue of the natiuitie, the other, of the precedent coniunction or oppoſition of the brightnes : the third, of the verification by the Animodar : the fourth, of the conception. The which beſides the vnprofitable and ſuperfluous labour, erre greatly, thinking to find out the tyme of the conception by the Animodar of *Ptolome*, the which experience from day to day ſheweth to be falſe, and that it hath no auncient Author to maintaine it, or hath made mention of thys newe doctrine, being full of contention and diſproued veritie.

¶ The Table of the time that the Childe dooth
remaine within the wombe of
his Mother.

fig	degr.	dayes			
	The Moone beeing vnder the Horrizon, reckon from the Ascendaunt.			The Moone being aboue the Horrizon, reckon from the seauenth.	
0	0	273	Indifferent abiding.	258	Little abiding.
0	12	274		259	
0	24	275		260	
1	6	276		261	
1	18	277		262	
2	0	278		263	
2	12	279		264	
2	24	280		265	
3	6	281		266	
3	18	282		267	
4	0	283		268	
4	12	284		269	
4	24	285		270	
5	6	286		271	
5	18	287		272	
5	29	288	Long abiding.	273	

CHAP. III.
*The manner to sette downe perfectlie the
said figure verified.*

Hauing put to the poynt of the first house, the degree & minutes of the Moone of the time of the
conception, take the ouerthwart ascentions of the
said degrees and minutes : take out afterward 90.
degrees of the sayd ascentions, and adde thereto 360. degrees, if otherwise the substraction cannot be made : that
which remaineth, shalbe the right ascentions of the highest poynt of the circle Meridian, the which search in the

A 3   table

table of the right afcentions, in the booke of *Alphonce*, or of *Iohn de Regiomonte*, &c. and put to the poynt of the tenth houfe, the degrees & minutes of the figne you find, aunfwering to the right number of the faid right afcentions. The poynt of the fourth is alwaies againft the figne and degree of the tenth : likewife the poynt of the feauenth, to the poynt of the firft. The other houfes fufficed, take the Ephemerides, becaufe they doe not defire exact calculation, feeing that the moft part of the Aftrologians, defire more to take of the equall portion of the Eclipfe then of the horizontall fect.

For to know the exact hower of the faid figure, verifie firft the fayd right afcentions of the Meridian, and take from them the right afcentions of the Sunne, that which remaineth turne into howers and minutes, gyuing to xv. degrees one hower, to euery degree foure minutes of an hower. &c. as we haue fayde before. At thys hower you muft newly count the moouing of the Moone, and of the Sunne, & of the other Planets : and vpon thys figure you muft ground the parts and iudgements Aftronomicall.

Chap. IIII.
Of the partes of Natiuities.

AFter you haue well fought the Planets in the fayd figure verified, you muft confider their aboue certaine proportions of the Planets and partes of the heauen, taken of theyr diftances, as followeth.

The parts concerning the fignifications of the firft Houfe.

The part of the qualitie of the lyfe, is taken by the diftance of Iupiter from Saturne, counting as much fpace from the afcendant, as when the natiuity is by day : for when it is by night, they take it to the cotrary, the diftance of Saturne vnto Iupiter, folowing the natural order of the fignes, counting likewife as much fpace fince the afcendant.

The

The part of lyfe by day and by night, is taken of the degree of the precedent coniunction, or opposition of the lights vnto the Moone, counting from the ascendant.

The part of the Spirite (many do call the part of earthly things and secrets, the other, the part of things to come, the others, the part of the Sun) in the day, frō the Moone vnto the Sunne, from the ascendant, in the night to the contrary.

The part of the vnderstanding, by the day, is frō Mercurie vnto Mars, from the ascendant, at night to the contrarie.

Of the second House.

The part of Fortune by the day, is from the Sunne vnto the Moone, from the ascendant, at night to the contrarie. *Ptolome* doth take it as much by day as by night, from the Sunne vnto the Moone.

The part of the goods aswell by day as by night, is from the Lord of the second house, vnto the said second house, taken vpon the quality of the Eclipse, frō the ascendant.

Of the third.

The part of brothers, by the day, is from Saturne vnto Iupiter, from the ascendant, at night to the contrary.

The part of the loue of bretheren, by the day, is from the Sunne vnto Saturne, from the ascendant, at night to the contrary. If Saturne bee vnder the beames of the Sunne, take Iupiter in his place.

Of the fourth.

The part of father, by the day, is from the Sun vnto Saturne, from the ascendant, at night to the contrary. Thys same is like the loue of bretheren: then if Saturne be vnderneath the beames of the Sun, in his place take Iupiter.

The part of inheritances and possessions, by day and by night, is from Saturne to the Moone, from the ascendant.

The part of fortune in tillage and sowing, by day and by night, is from Venus vnto Saturne, from the ascendant.

Of

Of the fift.

The part of Infants, is as the part of the qualitie of the lyfe.

The part of male chyldren by day and by night, is from the Moone vnto Iupiter, and is numbred from the ascendant.

The part of daughters, by day and by night, is from the Moone vnto Venus, and is taken from the ascendant.

Of the sixt.

The part of diseases inseperable, in the day, is the distaunce of Saturne vnto Mars, and it is cast from the degree ascendant, and in the night from Mars, which is contrary.

The part of seruaunts, by day and by night, from Mercurie vnto the Moone, is from the ascendant.

The part of pryson and captiuity by day, from the lord of the place of the Sunne, vnto the Sunne, and is reckoned from the ascendant. By night, from the Lorde of the place of the Moone, vnto the Moone.

If the Sunne by day, or the Moone by night, be in theyr proper houses or exaltations, they shall be signifiers of thys part.

Of the seauenth.

The part of the marriage of men, by day and by night, from the Sunne vnto Venus, is from the ascendant.

The part of the marriage of women, by day & by night, from Venus to Saturne, is from the ascendant.

The part of marriage common to men & to women, by day and by night, is from Venus vnto the poynt of the seauenth house, accounting from the ascendant.

The part of kindred, by day and by night, from Saturne vnto Venus, is from the ascendant.

The part of discord & agreement, by day, is from Mars to Iupiter from the ascendant : by night to the contrary.

Of

Of the eight.

The part of death , by day and by night , from the Moone vnto the degree of the eyght houfe, taken vpon the equalitie of the Eclipfe accounting from the place of Saturne.

The part of the mortall Planet by day is from the Lord of the afcendant, vnto the Moone, from the afcendant, by night to the contrary.

The part of the perrillous yeere of death, or pouerty, or of any other mif-fortune by day, and by night, is from Saturne vnto the Lord of the fore-faid coniunction or oppofition of the light, from the afcendant.

The part of all enuies, by day, is from Saturne vnto Mars, by night to the contrary, accounting frō the place of Mercurie.

Of the ninth.

The part of fayth and of religion, by day , is from the Moone vnto Mercurie, from the afcendant , by night to the contrary.

The part of waies by land by day and by night, is from the Lord of the ninth vnto the ninth, taken vpon the equalitie of the Eclipfe, from the afcendant.

The part of trauaile by water by day , is from Saturne vnto the fifteenth degree of Cancer, from the afcendant, at night to the contrary.

If Saturne doe meete in the fayde fifteenth degree of Cancer, he fhall be fignifier of this part, with the afcendant.

Of the tenth.

The part of nobilitie, by day, is from the Sunne vnto the nineteenth degree of Aries, accounting from the afcendant, by night, from the Moone vnto the third degree of Taurus. If the Moone by night be in the faid degree of Taurus, or the Sunne by day in the faid degree of Aries,

       they

they shall be signifiers of the said part.

The part of gouernment by day, is from Mars vnto the Moone from the ascendant, by night to the contrary.

The part of Magistrates, as the part of the vnderstanding, written vpon the first house.

The part of conquest & victorie, as the parte of father.

The part of suddaine aduauncement, by day, is from Saturne vnto the part of Fortune, from the ascendant, by night to the contrary; If Saturne be burned, take in hys place Iupiter.

The part of estimation, by day and by night, is from Mercurie vnto the Sunne, accounting from the ascendant.

The part of gouernment and feates of warre, by day, is from Mars vnto Saturne, from the ascendant, by night to the contrary.

The part of the profession and action, by day and by night, is from Saturne vnto the Moone frō the ascendant.

The part of honour proceeding of the profession, by day and by night, is from the degree of the Sunne, vnto the degree of the tenth house, from the ascendant.

The part of the industry of the hands, by day, is from Mercurie to Venus, from the ascendant, by night to the contrary.

The part of the feate of Merchandize, by day, is from the part of the sonne, vnto the part of Fortune, from the ascendant, by night to the contrary.

The part of felicitie, and profit, by day, is from the part of Fortune vnto Iupiter, from the ascendant, by night to the contrary.

The part of the mother, by day, is from Venus vnto the Moone, from the ascendant, by night to the contrary.

Of the eleuenth.

The part of friendes, by day and by night, is from Mercurie to the Moone, from the ascendant.

The part of praise, by day is from Iupiter, vnto Venus from the ascendant, by night to the contrarie.

The

The part of honourable companies, by day, is from the part of Fortune vnto the Sunne, from the ascendant, by night to the contrary.

Of the twelfth.

The part of enemies, by day & by night, is from the lord of the xij. house, vnto the said xij. taken vpon the equalitie of the Eclipse, from the ascendant.

The second part of enemies, as the part of diseases inseperable, written in the sixt house.

The part of paine, trauaile and affliction, by day and by night, is frō the part of the spirite, vnto the part of fortune.

CHAP. V.
Of the latitudes and aspects of the Planets.

Hauing applyed the Planets in the saide figure, and ordained as we haue said in the former chapter, the parts proceeding of the proportions of the said Planets, you must consequently draw out of the Ephemerides theyr latitudes, & put apart all the aspects which is among them, and towardes the said parts and xij. houses; also the radiations, after the last proposition of the booke of Directions of *Iohn de Regiomonte*: vpon the which note, that the aspects opposites, haue alwaies diuers latitudes to them of their Planets, although they keepe the same number. As if Saturne had two degrees of latitude septentrionall, his opposition hath two degrees of latitude meridionall. The quadrant aspect hath no latitude, for it falleth alwaies vpon the Eclipse.

The Trine aspect, retaineth the halfe of the number of the latitude, in contrary part: for if d Planet haue one degree of latitude meridionall, his trine shall haue thirtie minutes of latitude septentrionall. The Sextile retaineth the same side, with the halfe of the number. You must also note, that these aspects of Saturne and of Iupiter, doo not extend but vnto nine degrees, or for the most longest vnto twelue; thofe of Mars vnto eyght, or for the moft part to tenne. The Sunne extendeth his beames to xv. degrees, Venus and Mercurie almoft to eyght. The Moone vnto twelue, the head & taile of the Dragon, likewife extend their forces vnto twelue degrees.

Moreouer, it is to be noted, that the oppofition is a plaine afpect and perfect enmity: the Quadrate of leſſe enmity: the Trine of perfect loue: the Sextile of imperfect loue. That which alwaies receiueth exception in Iupiter and Venus, (of the which oppofites and quadrate afpects) profit the Sunne & the Moone with reception, or without reception, and to others alfo with reception.

CHAP. VI.

Of the fortunes and infortunes of the Planets,
and parts of Heauen.

AFter this, you muft confider the forces & weakeneſſe of the Planets, parts and Houfes, and conferring the ones fignifications with the other, you muft collect the fortunes and infortunes of euerie place, as followeth.

Heere followeth the infortunes.

The Planets and other places of the Heauen, be called vnfortunate, when they be burned vnder the beames of the Sunne. Burnings are called Saturne and Iupiter, when betweene them & the Sunne they haue leſſe then twelue degrees. Mars when he is burned of the Sunne, hath at the leaft xj. degrees and a halfe. Venus and Mercurie, when they be neere the Sunne, xj. degrees. The Moone when fhe is not burned, by xiij. And yet you find other termes, when you will take a Planet for to giue the yeeres. Then the three fuperiours are efteemed burnt, becaufe they are neere the Sunne by xv. degrees, and if they be occidental. For when they be orientall vnto tenne degrees, they are burnt from the tenne vnto xv. vnder the beames. Venus and

and Mercurie occidentall neere to the Sunne by seauen degrees, or orientall by fiue, be burned, from thence vnto twelue vnder the beames. The Moone neere by twelue degrees is burnt, from thence vnto xv. vnder the beames. And you must note, that the saide accidents are not hurtfull when they fall in the signes of Aries, and of the Lyon.

Vnfortunate also are the Planets, when they goe backwarde, and when they bee ioyned with Saturne or with Mars: or when they receiue euill aspects of them.

When they are ioyned with any fixed starre of violent nature.

When they are in their detriments or fallings, (that is to say) in places opposite to their houses or exaltations.

When they are in their declining houses.

When they are first standers, (that is to say) when they be in the degree and minute wherein incontinently they beginne to goe backward.

When they are in the way of burning, which beginne at the 19. degree of Libra, and end in the third degree of Scorpio.

When they be with the tayle of the Dragon.

When they are ioyned with a backward Planet, or otherwise vnfortunate.

When they are Peregrines, without beeing receiued. They are called Peregrins, when they haue no dignitie or place where they be. Of the reception we will speake afterwards.

When they be meridionall descendents.

When any of the three superiours are occidentall, or Venus & Mercurie orientall, when they be in euil aspects of the Sunne.

When they doe not regard any other Planet.

When they be opposits to the Lord of the signe where they be.

When they be sette, (that is to say) betweene two euill Planets, although they haue 30. degrees of distance.

When they be in euill houses or termes.

When

When they be in the twelfth ſigne of theyr principall houſes.

When they be vnder the Horrizon in the day, or aboue the Horrizon in the night : if they be Diurnes, as Saturne, Iupiter, and the Sunne.

When they be aboue the Horrizon in the day, and beneath at night. If they be Noćturnes, as. Mars, Venus, Mercurie, and the Moone.

When they be in ſignes and degrees feminine, they be maſculines, or in ſignes and degrees maſculine, they bee feminines. Feminines are Venus and the Moone, Mercurie and Androgine, the others are maſculines.

When they be in degrees which are called *Azimena*, or in degrees ſtincking, darke, or ſmokie. That which is marked in the Ephemerides, in the table of the dignities of the Planets,

Infortunes particuler to the Moone.

When ſhe decreaſeth.

When ſhe is within the eyght Houſe, out of her principall dignities.

When ſhe is within the ſeauenth, and that as to the life. And as for any other ſignifications ſhe is not infortunate in the ſeauenth.

When ſhe is in the xix. degree of a ſigne.

When ſhe is ſlack in her courſe, (that is to vnderſtand) when ſhee goes in twenty-foure bowers, leſſe then thyrteene degrees and xi. minutes.

The fortunes of the Planets.

Fortunate be the Planets, and other places of Heauen, when they be in angles, or at the leaſt in houſes ſuccéeding.

When they be in a good aſpećt of Iupiter, or of Venus, or at the leaſt in euill, with reception

When

When they bee ioyned to the Sunne within sixteene mynutes.

When they be in a good aspect of the Sunne, of the Moone, or of Mercurie fortunate.

When they be ioyned with any fixed starre of a louing nature.

When they be directs, or at the least, in the second station, (that is to vnderstand) when they be in degree and minute, in the which beginneth incontinently the direction.

When they be within theyr proper houses or exaltations.

When they be in theyr triplicities and termes together, or triplicity and face together.

When they be in houses, wherein they naturally take pleasure, as Mercurie in the ascendant, the Moone in the third, Venus in the fift, Mars in the sixt, the Sunne in the ninth, Iupiter in the eleuenth, and Saturne in the twelfth.

When they be in any of theyr dignities, or if they be peregrines, when they be receiued. Receiued; that is, the Planets, which receiue aspect of him, which in their place hath at the least foure dignities, the which reception is fortunate, when shee is made of a good aspect.

At all times the receptions of Iupiter and Venus be alwaies fauourable, although they be not made of good aspects.

When they mount to the highest part of their Circles.

When they be septentrionals, principally ascendants.

When any of the three Superiours is orientall, or Venus and Mercurie occidentall.

When they beginne to goe from the beames of the Sunne.

When they be in Houses or termes of fauourable Planets.

When they be aboue the Horrizon in the day, or vnder the Horrizon in the night, if they be Diurnes.

When

of tyme that doth regard it: If it be in the nynth, eygth, or seuenth house, it may also be the giuer of life, if it be in a Masculine signe, and not in a Feminine: in other places it cannot be the giuer of life, but by constraint. It is alwaies necessarie for such an acte, that the giuer of time regard the giuer of life, otherwise, the sayd giuer of life shall be as person that hath good will to doo his friend good, & hath not wherewithall; And so when the Sunne shall be without aspect of any giuer of time, you must leaue it there, & goe to the Moone, which may giue the life within the first house, in the signe Masculine or Feminine, and within the tenth, eleuenth, seuenth, fourth, fifth, second and third house, in signes Feminines and not Masculines, receiuing aspect of any giuer of time. If the Moone haue not all the sayde conditions, you must come to the degree ascendant, if the natiuitie be coniunctionall (Coniunctionall is sayed the natiuitie, before the which lastly the lights haue beene conioyned) and if the sayde degree receiue aspect of his gyuer of time, he shall be gyuer of life: otherwise not. Wherefore you must examine the part of Fortune, the which shall giue life in the Angles and houses succeeding, with the aspect of the giuer of time, otherwise you must come to the degree, to the which lastly the lights haue beene conioyned: the which within the Angles or houses succeeding shall be giuer of life, if hee receiue aspect of his giuer of tyme.

It is heere necessary that the giuer of time haue dignitie of house, or of exaltation in places of the part of Fortune, and of the sayd degree coniunctionall. By this order you must seeke the gyuer of life, when the natiuitie is coniunctionall. When she is preuentionall, (Preuentionall is sayed, afore the which lastly the lights haue beene opposites) after you haue considered the Sunne and the Moone, you must consequentlie contemplate the place of Fortune, more than the degree ascendant, and lastly the degree of the oppositions of the lights, & see that it haue 2. degrees in the opposition, one of them of the Sunne, and

the

the other of the Moone. The Aftrologians commaund to confider it, that at the time of the oppofition it hath beene in the firft houfe, or elswhere aboue the Horizon.

When the Natiuitie is nocturniall, we followe the fame order, (except that firft we confider the Moone, fecondly the Sunne, &c.) This gyuer of life, when either by directi-on, or by profection, or by other way, meete any euill a-fpect of the infortunes, or of the ftarres fixed of vyolent nature, or any of the notable coniunctions, or Eclipfes of the lightes, it caufeth then fome ficknefe, and very fud-daynly bringeth death, when the Fortunes doo not inter-mingle the fauourable beames.

Chap. IX.

Of the giuer of yeeres, called of the Arabians
Alcocoden.

THE gyuer of time or giuer of yeeres, is the fame that hath dignitie of houfe, exaltation, triplicitie, or tearme in the place where is the giuer of life. As if the Sunne were in the xj. in the figne of Sagitarius, (there where he may be gyuer of life,) and Iupiter were in the figne of Aquarius, he fhall regarde the Sunne of the Sextile afpect, and looke that he haue dignitie of the houfe in the figne of the Sunne, he fhalbe giuer of yeeres. It is then neceffary, that thefe two thinges concurre toge-ther, to the end that one Plannet be giuer of yeeres, that is to fay, that he hath dignitie neuertheles of tearme (for the dignitie of face is not fufficient enough for one fo great effect) in figne and degree, in the which fhall be the giuer of life, and that he regarde the fayd giuer of life, of one a-fpect or other.

This gyuer of time, well lodged vpon the point of An-gles, gyueth him olde yeeres, in points of the houfes fuc-ceeding: is meanes, is Cadants, is fmalneffe, and for as much as he fhall be long from the beginnings of the faid houfes, fo much the more or leffe hee muft diminifh the number of his olde yeeres, meanes, and fmalnes, after

C 2   the

the difference taken of the next houſes with the difference of yeeres. And firſt of all if it be within any angle of
heauen, not alwayes to the firſt poynt, you muſt proceede
alſo, and take in the firſt place the diſtance of the ſayd angle, and of the next houſe ſucceeding. Note afterwarde,
how many degrees the ſaid giuer of yeeres is frō the point
of the angle. Then take the difference of his olde yeeres
and meanes, multiply this difference by the number of
the ſayd elongment, and part it by the diſtance of the ſayd
angle, & of the houſe ſucceeding: that which reſteth, take
for the exact number of the yeres of life, promiſed by the
ſaide giuer of yeeres. If hee be within any houſe, ſucceeding out of the points and beginnings of the ſame, you
muſt firſt take the diſtance of the houſe ſucceeding, and
of the next Cadant: then note how many degrees the ſaid
giuer of yeeres ſhall be elonged from the point of the ſaid
houſe ſucceeding; afterward take the difference of yeres,
meanes and ſmalnes, the which multiply by the ſecond
number, and part it by the firſt : the reſidue ſhall be the
time of life which was promiſed by the ſaid giuer of yeres.
If it bee in Cadant houſes it ſhall be vppon the points of
them, or after, he giueth but onely ſmall yeeres : Except
when he is within 5. degrees neere to the point of the ſaid
angles, & then you muſt reckon as it followeth. Take the
difference of the olde yeeres, and ſmalnes of the Plannets
that giueth the yeres, and deuide them into 5. parts; afterward looke in which of the ſaid 5. degrees ſhal be the ſaid
Plannet. For if it be in the firſt and moſt neere the poynt
of the angle, (that is to ſay) if he be elonged from the ſaid
angle one degree onely, then is it conuenient to take out
of his old yeeres, one of the ſayd 5. parts : if he be elonged
by 2. degrees, you muſt take out 2. parts : if he be elonged
3. degrees, you muſt ſubſtract 3. parts, &c. You muſt note
that the Moone in the viij. giues but ſmall yeeres. And
that the Sunne within the 9. and Iupiter in the 11. and Venus in the 5. and Mercury by the whole aſcendant, and
the Moone in the 3. giue their olde yeeres as perfectly, as

if

if they were vpon the points of the angles : For they be
places wherein principally they doo reioyce. Iupiter,
Venus, and Mercury within the 9. giue theyr yeeres indifferent : and the Moone in the 11. giues them old. Mars
in the 6. and Saturne in the 12. they are indifferent, becaufe in the faide places they greatly delight themfelues :
wherefore if they were not euill, they woulde there giue
olde yeeres.

Vppon this propofe it is conuenient alfo to note , that
one burnt Plannet cannot bee a giuer of yeeres : and the
Moone in the prime of the beames of the Sunne, cannot
giue life nor time. If a Plannet, which otherwife may be a
giuer yeeres, bee burnt in his proper houfe or exaltation,
receiuing there the Sunne, caufeth the Sunne to take the
charge to be the giuer of yeeres. If it come to paffe that
the Sunne or the Moone be in their proper houfes or exaltations, they may be giuers of life & time together, with
out neede to defire afpect of any other Plannet. If one
place being fignificator of life, haue many giuers of yeres,
wee will take him that hath moft dignities in the fame
place, and if they be equall in dignities wee will take hym
that hath his afpect moft whole , and his beames moft
neereft the fayd giuer of life. If they finde two or three
or many giuers of life, that haue their giuers of yeres, they
muft alwayes confider and direct, as the firft and principall, following the yeeres of the Plannets.

Olde yeeres.	Meane yeeres.	Small yeeres.	Of	
57	43	30	Saturne.	♄
79	45	12	Iupiter.	♃
66	40	15	Mars.	♂
120	69	19	Sol	☉
82	45	8	Venus.	♀
76	48	20	Mercury.	☿
108	66	25	Luna.	☽

C H A P. X.
*Of them that augment and diminish the number
of the sayd yeeres.*

THey which augment the number of the sayd yeres,
are Iupiter, Venus, the Sunne, the Moone, & Mercurie fortified; the which fortunatly regarding the
gyuer of yeeres, with an amiable aspect adding to
their small yeeres, (that is to vnderstand) the Sunne x. and
ix. Venus viij. the Moone xxv. &c. Likewise If the gyuer of time be conioyned with any fixed starre of amiable
nature, it taketh of the said starre the number of the small
yeeres of the Plannet, of the which the said starre holdeth
his nature, If the said Plannets regard the giuer of time
with an euill aspect with reception, they adde as before,
which they doo not when they haue no reception : Except Iupiter and Venus, that in euery sort of aspects, with
reception or without reception, alwayes adding to theyr
small yeeres, for to see that the gyuer of tyme be not Saturne or Mars, towards the which the reception is necessary, if the aspect be of enmitie.

The sayd Plannets euill placed and infortunate, in the
place of the whole small yeeres, in adding the halfe, or the
third, or fourth part , or certaine number of monethes, of
weekes, or of dayes, according to the greatnesse or smal-
nesse of theyr infelicitie. The amiable aspects of ill fortunes, with reception , giue theyr yeeres small : without
reception, they doo neither good nor euill. If the giuer of
yeeres be retrogarde or meridionall descending, or in hys
fall or detryment, or in the way burned, that taketh from
it the fift part of that which hee had giuen beeing otherwise disposed. That which happened also to the 3. superiour Planets, when they be occidentall, & to the Moone
when she decreaseth, and when shee is in the xx. and ix.
degree of a signe, and when she is slack in her course. The
Sunne regarding the Moone with the aspects of enmitie
without reception diminished. Saturne, Mars, or Mercurie

curie depriued, looking to the euill aspect of the giuer of
light they take away the number of their small yeeres: Except they recouer ; For then by opposition they doe but
halfe the euill : By quadrate aspect,they diminish but the
fourth part. The tayle of the Dragon taken from the
Moone xij. yeeres , I haue found it often by experience,
that the fortunes(that is to vnderstand,Iupiter & Venus)
or the Sunne and the Moone, and Mercurie fortunate in
the first house,or neere to the giuer of life,adding to their
small yeeres, although they doe not regarde the giuer of
time : and to the contrarie, that the infortunes in the sayd
places, take away the small yeeres, without regarding the
saide giuer of time. Except when they were well honoured in the sayd places , or when they were Lordes of the
Natiuities.

Chap. XI.
Of the Lordes of the Natiuitie.

YOu must take the Lord of the Natiuitie, out of the
places of the which we haue taken the giuer of life,
(that is to vnderstand)of the place of the Sunne and
of the Moone, of the degree ascendant of the part of
Fortune,and of the degrees of the precedent coniunction
or opposition of lightes. Of all these places likewise it is
to be considered , what Plannet hath most dignities, for
he shall be Lord of the Natiuitie, that which the giuer of
yeeres shall signifie the tyme of our life,according to the
scituation & felicitie or infelicitie, as we haue before sayd
of the giuer of yeeres. And if the one giue more than the
other,you must take the difference of both, and the halfe
ad or diminish:according as shall be necessarie.

Of

The Signes.	
The house of the Planettes.	5
Exaltation.	
The triplicitie of the Planettes.	3
The termes of the Planettes.	2
The faces of the Planettes.	1
When the Planettes haue no dignities. — Perigren.	
The hurtes.	
The falls.	

*Of the vnderstanding and manners of
a Man.*

HOW to knowe the felicitie or infelicitie of the Spirite,& the nature of the fame,you muſt looke in the place of Mercurie and of the Moone, the Planet that in theſe two places hath moſt digni-ties, ſhall be ſignifier of the ſpirite. The which if it be Sa-turne well diſpoſed, ſhall ſignifie the man of a great and profound knowledge, of good counſell, and of good gra-uitie or a ſtrong opinion : cloſe, ſecrete, ſolitarie, diſſem-bling his good and euill, a louer of iuſt men, and of good age : reioycing vpon the treaſures , heritages and labou-rings ; holding diſcourſe of antiquities and of great af-fayres, admirator of buildings. Sometimes a little merrie, incontinent ſadde : ſometymes laughing or murmuring by himſelfe alone, a lyttle ſlothfull, a little enuious , and not alwaies keeping hys promiſe. If he be vnfortunate, he ſhall be noted enuious, ſadde, ſolitarie, fearefull, mel-lancholie, faint-harted, a raylor, iealous, a malefactor, e-uill, a blaſphemer, a lyer & decciuer, a Vſurer, & holder of opinions : reiecting the counſell of others : fearing that all the world doth deceiue hym : vnciuill, a villaine,a ſlo-uine, diſhoneſt, flying the company of men vnleſſe it be to deceiue them,and to draw any profite,hauing no other friend but his villainous gayne, vſing ſomtimes ſorcery.

Iupiter ſignifier of the ſpirite,well diſpoſed, ſhewes the man ſweete, curteous,honeſt, gracious, amiable,faithfull, pittifull, liberall, of good behauior, of good hart & good loue: following nobleneſſe and all honeſty : louing God, abounding in friendes, dreaming alwaies vpon ſome ver-tuous thing, and withdrawes himſelfe ſometimes ſolitary, to thinke vpon ſome goodnes : vſing in all and by all hys affayres,a great equitie, prudence and modeſtie , hauing great courage to accompliſh. If hee be vnfortunate of himſelfe, and not to meete with other ſtarres,in the place

D   of

of good loue, hee will giue ſometimes fooliſhnes in the place of honeſty, pryde in the place of liberalitie, prodigalitie in the place of louing good will, doth yeeld hym an hypocrite, ſeeming to follow nobleneſſe, when indeed he will diſpraiſe all the world : in the place of honeſtie , it wyll make hym dreame of tyranny.

If the ſaid Iupiter be vnfortunate of other Planets and not of hymſelfe, he taketh all theyr vices , and couereth them with his ſayde vertues in manner of an euill hypocrite. If Mars well fortunate be the ſaid ſignificator, hee ſhall cauſe the man to be of a high courage, hardy, irefull, furious, a hazarder, a conducter of warres , & the firſt in buſineſſe, and onely in deedes and cogitations gyuen to armes : ſtrong, ſtubberne and mightie, truſting too much to his owne puiſſaunce, not fearing any perrill, and bleſſed in all hys deedes. If he be vnfortunate, it maketh the man tymerous, a theefe, a lyer, blaſphemer , mutenous, cruell, a murtherer, hardy, proude, arrogant, not to be borne withall, deſpyſing hys owne proper goods, and the goods of other, vſing force and violence againſt hys Parents, and againſt all the worlde : a diuiliſh man, without ſhame, without counſell, without vertue , without loue, without any feare or reuerence of God, furious, ſeditious, gyuen and prompt to all miſchiefe.

If the Sunne be ſignificator in his good diſpoſition, it makes the man mannerly, wiſe, prudent, of good counſell, a louer of noblenes, following glory and honour, gyuen to iuſtice and gouernments of Townes and Citties , louing hunting, worthy, and of great eſtimation. If it be vnfortunate, it ſheweth great pride, exceſſiue ambition, and tyrannie, and doth nouriſh the thought.

If Venus ſignifie the qualitie of the ſpirite in good diſpoſition, it maketh the man pleaſant, merry , dauncing, laughing, content, amiable, gracious, of good conuerſation, and a little ielous. If vnfortunate, it maketh the man frowning, and too merry , of euill maintenaunce, vſing diſhoneſt words, giuen to voluptuouſnes, and ielous of

that

that which belongeth not vnto him.

If Mercurie bee fortunate, it gyues good vnderstan-ding, good memorie, great perseuerance, great subtiltie of spyrite, good discourse of reason, full of wit, very apt to know the Mathematicals, and the secretes of nature; it makes the man a Poet, an Orator, well spoken, writing well, and a great trader. If it be euill disposed, it makes him presumpteous, of little knowledge, with great estima-tion of his person, inconstant, a lyer, a mocker, a decei-uer ordinarily, fine, fantasticall, and vicious.

If it be the Moone that is fortunate, shee maketh him that is borne, pacified, modest, of good hart, or good will, and easie to endure any thing that one will doe. Vnfortu-nate doth shew inconstancie, lightnes of spyrite, faint-har-ted, prodigall, faythlesse. If the sayde signifiers, are not greatly fortunate or vnfortunate, it is conuenient to re-bate the sayde significations good and vicious, after the qualitie of theyr good and euill dispositions.

If any Planet be participant in the signification of the manners, or if it haue great communication of aspect with the principall significator, then considering the vices and vertues of him, that (according to his good or euill dis-position) wee doe ioyne them to him which gyueth the principall. As if Saturne well disposed, be principal sig-nificator, and Mars infortunate be participant, or regarde Saturne of one whole aspect with reception, then it is con-uenient to mingle some little of the nature of Mars vnfor-tunate, with the significations of Saturue fortunate.

The Astrologians doe aduertise vs, that if the Lord of the ascendant be well placed, and the saide significator of manners euill disposed, you must more consider vppon that which the Lord of the ascendant signifieth, then vp-pon that which the said significator doth promise. More-ouer, they consider more particulerly, the place of Mer-curie and of the Moone, and the aspect which they re-ceiue. If Mercurie be in the ascendant, it maketh the Man ingenious, and of great and profounde knowledge,

a great

a great Phyloſopher, a Mathematician, an Orator, a Poet, a Diuine; principally whē he is in the place in the which Saturne hath at the leaſt 4. dignities, or when he receiues aſpeƈt of Saturne.

Mercury in the twelfth, recciuing aſpeƈt of the Moone, hath very neere as great force for to giue wit and knowledge, as if he were in the firſt. And where that Mercurie is, if he regard the Moone, and both two, or the one or the other, regard the aſcendant or the Lord of the aſcendant, thys is ſigne of a good and ſubtile ſpyrite. And if Saturne, Iupiter and Mars, or other Planets, do communicate to him theyr fauorable beames, if they mingle theyr good vertues, if they regarde the euill aſpeƈt, they intermingle theyr vices : except Iupiter and Venus, which of euill aſpeƈt doe neuer anoy them, and leſſe when he hath reception.

If the Sunne be temporall light, it may ſignifie the quality of the ſpyrite with the Moone and Mercurie in the forme aboue ſayd. If Mercurie be occidentall within the houſe or exaltation of the Sunne, hauing aſpeƈt of the Moone, or of the aſcendant, or of his Lord, it is the foueraigne ſigne of good and high ſpirits, of men of al knowledge, gyuen to great enterpriſes and vertues, as Poets, Orators, Mathematicians, Counſellers, Adminiſtrators of Common-weales, and Gouernours of Realmes : principally when hee is fortunate in euery angle of Heauen.

Mercurie within the ſeauenth houſe fortunate, giueth good vnderſtanding, and ripe iudgement : it maketh the man ſubtile, watchfull, and of good counſell, with great craft to gouerne his affayres. Mercurie in the ninth or third houſe, giueth knowledge and contemplation. The part of the vnderſtanding of the ſpyrite with theyr Lords fortunate, ſignifieth good ſpirits and good manners.

Mercurie in the ſigne of Piſces, doth not any way loue learning: the contrary happeneth, when he is in the ſigne of Virgo and of Gemini, by all the places of the figure of Heauen. Saturne within the houſes of Mercurie, is al-

waies

waies contemplatiue : Mars, a lyttle deceiuer. Mercurie within the houſes of Saturne fortunate, is alwaies ſtudious, within thoſe of Mars, he is full of euill words, and often falſe.

When the lyghts and ſignificators of manners ſhall be oppreſſed with ill fortune, the chylde ſhall be of a verie ſtrange and peruerſe nature. The Moone oppoſite to the Sunne, makes hym hate all men. If the Sunne and the Moone with the aſcendant and his Lorde, be all in feminine ſignes, the manners of hym ſhall be feminine, and he ſhal be a man of little hart. If they be in ſignes maſculine at the natiuitie of a woman, her deedes ſhal be manly, and ſhe ſhall be a woman of great enterpriſe.

If Venus be in the ſigne of the Lyon, or vnder the beames of the Sunne, or in coniunction or other aſpect of Mars, ſhe maketh that the man ſhal be ſuddainly ſtriken in loue. And if in that eſtate ſhee be within the firſt or tenth houſe, without any aſpect of Iupiter, hee ſhall be voluptuous without hauing ſhame ; and when ſhe ſhalbe in the ſigne of Scorpio, the aſpect of Iupiter towards Venus, gyueth alwaies chaſtitie, and loue of vertue.

Chap. XIII.
Of riches and pouertie.

FOR the riches and pouertie, it is conuenient firſt that you looke to the ſeconde houſe, for if ſhee and her Lord be fortuuate, we ſay that the chyld ſhall be rich, and if they be vnfortunate, he ſhall be poore on that ſide. Then afterward you muſt conſider the part of Fortune, the which with hys Lorde well diſpoſed, promiſeth great ſtore of goods, without other witnes. If they be euill diſpoſed, you muſt come to the parte of goods the which with his Lord fortunate enricheth, vnfortunate gyueth nothing. Likewiſe you muſt iudge of the part of felicity and of his Lord. And that thing which the other places ſignifie, you muſt alwaies haue recourſe to the na-

turall

turall ſignificator of riches, which is Iupiter, the which well placed and fortunate, gyueth goods in aboundance: principally if he be Lord of the natiuity, or Lorde of the hower, or of the aſcendant, or of the ſeconde houſe, or of the part of Fortune, or of the part of goods, or of the part of felicitie, or of temporall light, or of the tenth houſe, otherwiſe he gyueth nothing.

When the aboue-ſayde Significators ſhall be vnfortunate, the chylde cannot be rich, if the tenth houſe (of the which wee will ſpeake heereafter) doe not promiſe hym ſome good lucke. Men finde alſo often by experience, that when a Planet is within his own houſe or exaltation, or in hys ioy, (without beeing vnfortunate, or els where enuironed with the fortunes or theyr beames) that hee gyueth goods, although he be not Significator of riches. If in the fourth houſe be hys lord or other fortunate Planet, he promiſeth inheritaunces. If any fixed ſtarre of the firſt or ſecond greatnes be ioyned to the temporall lyght, or to the degree aſcendant, or to the poynts of the other angles, or to other Planets in the ſayd places placed, ſhe dooth rayſe the man of baſe eſtate, to great authority and honour: and if he be of the race of Princes, it will make hym a puiſſant Lord and King.

When a lyke Planet ſhall be Lord of the aſcendant, & of the ſecond houſe, the chylde ſhall be couetous of money & gayne, as that which happeneth when Capricorne is aſcendant. When the Lord of the ſecond houſe ſhal be within the firſt, the goods come without laboure. Likewiſe when the Lord of the ſecond houſe giueth ſtrength to the Lord of the aſcendant. When the Lorde of the aſcendant ſhall be in the ſecond, the goods ſhall not come without trauayle: nor whē the lord of the aſcendant ſhall gyue ſtrength to the Lord of the ſecond. Saturne, Mars, Mercurie depraued, the Sunne and the tayle of the Dragon lunarie, within the ſecond, deſtroy the man, and diſperſe his goods; except when they haue at the leaſt foure dignities, or when they be receiued. When the
Lord

Lord of the afcendant fhall regarde with euill afpect the fecond houfe, or the part of goods and of fortune, or their Lords, the chyld of hys owne proper will fhall difperfe his goods. If the Lord of the afcendant be vnfortunate in the fecond houfe, the chyld fhall be too large a giuer, and prodigall. If any mif-fortune haue domination vpon the afcendant, and in the feond, the chylde fhall be deftroyed by others, which fhall deftroy hys goods and robbe hym. When the fayde Significators of goods fhall be vnfortunate, the chyld fhall be all hys lyfe in payne and trauaile, without any aduauncement or profite.

Abraham Auenefie faith, that if the Lord of the fecond be burnt, and Iupiter euill difpofed, that the chyld fhalbe alwayes poore. And *Hermes* fayth : when the Lord of the profefsion (of the which we fhall fpeak in the 27. chap.) fhall be burnt, or retrogard, or in the fixt or xij. houfe, and not any Planet regarding the Moone, the chyld fhall feeke hys lyuing from doore to doore like a begger. Iupiter, Venus, and the head of the Dragon in the fecond, alwaies enrich. Venus in the fift promifeth fome good. The Sunne in the nynth fortunate, gyueth benefices, or other goods of the fide of the men of the Church. Mars in the fixt well difpofed, gyueth good or nourifhment to Beaftes, and exercife of Phificke. The Sunne in the figne of Leo, will neuer fuffer the child to be poore.

Foure Planets in their fals or detryments, do fhewe great miferies, as it was in the natiuite of Iohn Duke of Saxony, who was také prifoner of Charles the 5. Thys good Duke had 3. Planets in their detryments, and one Perigren.

CHAP. XIIII.
By what meanes riches and pouerty commeth.

HAuing well noted the places which promife and bring riches, in regarding the fituation of the faid fignificators, we wyll know by what means ought to come the good and the euill. For if the fignificator be in the firft houfe receiued and fortunate, it eafily inricheth the perfon by hys induftry and proper labour : and if he be in the fayd place vnfortunate, it is that his induftry and labour doth profit hym nothing ; and the fooner from thence to loffe and damage.

If

If he be in the ſecond houſe well diſpoſed, it profiteth to talke with _Merchants_, and lend merchandize & money, and of them make gaine. And if he be there euil diſpoſed, the ſayd buſines bringeth great damages. If he be within the thirde houſe fortunate, it bringeth the goods from the ſide of Brothers and Siſters, and Coſins & alyes, or frō the ſide of the men of the Church in taking charge of theyr affayres : or to traffique heere and there about his Country. If he be in the 4. wel placed, he is inriched of inheritances & goods of our fathers & predeceſſors, of laborings & tilling of ground, of houſes, & oftentimes doth meete with treaſure. If it be within the fift, it profits to be a good Dauncer, a good Player, to bee braue, gracious, pleaſant and delightfull, and ſometimes to be voluptuous : alwayes well, becauſe of God-fathers and God-mothers, and of theyr proper chyldren ; or becauſe of gyfts, or to make ſome voyage and doe ſome embaſſage. Thoſe things that come appertaining to brauery and volupteouſneſſe, and making ready delicates, odours & perfumes, of thys houſe they very ſuddainly draw theyr profite. If the ſayd ſignificator be in the ſixt well placed, hee ſhall make his profite in nouriſhing, and buying and ſelling of Sheepe, muttons, and other ſmall beaſtes, or ſhall become rich by the diligence and faithfulneſſe of his ſeruaunts, or ſhall gaine by the exerciſe of Phiſicke. The Gaylors and others which haue the charge of pryſons, drawe oftentimes theyr profit from thys houſe.

If the ſignificator be in the ſeauenth fortunate, it promiſeth great good of the ſide of women, by marriages or like agreements : and oftentimes to haue pleaded & gayned his ſute in the law, or hauing beene in the warres and pilled the enemies. If it be in the eyght well diſpoſed, it gyueth great dowrie and great good, becauſe of women, and ſometimes heritages, of the which he ſhall not greatlie thinke of. If it be in the ninth fortunate, hee ſhalbe enriched of the goods of the church, or by traffique & traueling in ſtrange Countries.

If

If it be well in the tenth, he shall haue his profit of the side of Kings, Princes, and Lordes, and be made of them Gouernours of Townes, and honourable Officers; or be enriched by their owne vocation and profession.

If it be within the eleuenth in good disposition, he profiteth by reason of friendes, and by fauour of men in authoritie.

If it be in the twelueth, fortunate, it giueth gayne by nourishing and selling of Horses, Mares, Oxen, Kyne, Cammells, and other great beastes : or to haue charge of pryfonners : or of the persecution of enemies, with profitable victorie in the end ; As oftentimes it happeneth to some, which accusing others, and cannot prooue the crymes intended be condemned to make a good amendes to the partie : after all which persecution, the partie doth finde himselfe content.

Saturne by himselfe, enricheth by heritages & labours, nourishing of all Cattell, and with trading with auncient men, or with Countrey-men, Marriners, & other vilde men : in Corne, Wines, Oyles, Fysh, Oade, Rosen, Allum, Leather, Tyles, Stones, Plaister, Chalke, Lyme, and such merchandize.

Iupiter, by Offices, benefices, and busines of men of the Church, and all gaynes that are made without deceit. Except when he is infortunate, for then vnder the shaddow of vertue, he dooth his affaires craftilie.

Mars, by warres, sutes, or thefts, or by slaughter, and selling of Cattell : or if it be in aspect of Venus, by physicke.

The Sunne, by honourable offices, dignities & Lordships, by great credit, by charges to keepe and gather the money of Princes and Common-weales.

Venus, by musique, pleasure, grace and vertue, by brauery, by play, and sometimes by voluptuousnes, and somtime to serue some great Ladie.

Mercury, to speake well and write well, and to be very skilfull, to be a Secretarie, a Register, a Poet, an Oratour,

E   and

and a good aduocate, to be a Geometrician, Arethmetrici-an, Aſtrologian, and a good trader. The moone for voy-ages, nauigation, wandring, and trading in far Countries, to haue the chardge of ſmall affaieres of the common wealth.

If the ſaid Significator be vnfortunat in the ſame places, they bring dammage and intereſtes, and if they be within the houſes of Saturne, Iupiter or other planets, wee iudge the profit & intereſt after the nature of Saturne, Iupiter, and other planets which ſhalbe lords of the ſame places.

Cʜᴀᴘ. XV.

Of the time when the riches and dam-
mages ſhall come.

THé ſayde riches ſhall come, when the Significators of goodes ſhall meete by direction, in body or in aſpects of amitie. As if Venus in ſome natiuitie promiſe goodes, they ſhall come when Venus by direction shall touche the place of Iupiter, or the degree of the ſecond houſe, or the part of fortune, or their good aſpects: Likewiſe you muſt iudge of dama-ges in goodes. For when a ſignificator of damages and intereſtes doth meete by directiō a ſignificator of goods, or his aſpects of enmitie, then certainly comes the loſſe and damage. As when Saturne or Mars meete Iupiter in the parte of fortune, the parte of goodes and other places which ſignifie riches, the which alſo you muſt di-rect to the ſayd ill fortunes, or to their euill aſpect ſygnify-ing alwayes ſome loſſe.

By the reuolutions alſo you may know the time of good and euill fortune. For when Iupiter in the natiui-tie ſhalbe in the ſigne Libra well diſpoſed, alwayes and as many times, as you ſhall find him in the reuolution in the ſigne, in the ſame fortune certainlie he ſhall then bring the goodes that he promiſed, at the houre of the Nati-uitie.

To the contrarie, if hee be vnfortunate by Saturne or
Mars

Mars in the Natiuitie, alwayes and as many times as he shall be in the reuolution ouer againſt the ſayd vnfortunators, then the ſayd damage ſhall come in the ſort and manner as was ſignified in the natiuitie.

If the Significator of goodes be Orientall, the goodes come in youth, if it be Occidentall, in age. If it be in the firſt houſe hee ſhall be rich in his firſt age, if it be betweene the firſt and the tenth, vppon the time of twenty and ſeuen yeares. If it be in the tenth, betweene thirtye and fiue and thirtie. If it be betweene the tenth and ſeuenth, about fortie and fortie eight. If it be in the ſeuenth he ſhalbe rich in his old age. You muſt alſo looke to the three Lords of the triplicitie, and to euery Significator of goodes. For the firſt lord ſignifieth the firſt age, the ſecond of the time of thirtie or fortie yeares, the third the laſt age. Wherefore if the firſt lord of the triplicitie of one ſignificator of riches be fortunate, the ſayd goodes ſignified ſhall come at the firſt time : or if hee be vnfortunate, the damage then ſhall ſticke, by this meanes you may applie the other lordes, to the ages following, and according to the good or euill diſpoſition you muſt iudge of the fortune of euery one.

CHAP. XVI.
Of Bretheren.

MArs and Saturne within the thirde houſe out of their principall dignities and not receiued, ſignifieth that the childe ſhall haue no brother nor Siſter. And if they be in their principall dignities, or if they be fortunatly receiued, they may then giue ſome bretheren, but by reaſon of the which hee ſhall alwayes be in ſorrowe, ſtrife, and contentions. The taile of the Dragon or lunaris, maketh him ſee the death of his bretheren, when ſhee is in the thirde houſe. That doth the Lord of the ſayde houſe alſo, when hee is in the tenth or eight, and when he is burned or otherwiſe euilly diſpoſed.

E 2

If

If in the ix.be any Plannet well dignified,and the Lord of the third houſe be vnfortunate, his bretheren ſhall dye before him,if he doo not finde in the ſame houſe ſome fauourable Plannet,or if the Lord of the ſaide houſe be not amiably regarded of fortunes.

Iupiter, the Sunne, Venus , the head of the Dragon, the Moone , and Mercury, fortunate in the thirde houſe, doo giue many bretheren , happy , pacified and fortunate. Mars, regarding the ſaid houſe,or his Lord of euill aſpect, ſignifieth ſtrife and debate among the bretheren. That which ſignifieth alſo the Lord of the ſaid houſe, in the vij.and xij.And Mars oppoſite to the aſcendant,or to the Lord of the aſcendant,and to the temporall light, and when a like Plannet is Lord of the iij.and vij.or xij.houſe. The part of the amitie of bretheren with his Lord fortunate, ſignifieth concorde : vnfortunate, diſcorde among bretheren. The part of bretheren, and the third houſe, with their Lords in watry ſignes, denoteth many brethren and ſiſters: and if they be fortunate,they ſignifie concorde and good loue together : vnfortunate, denoteth the contrarie.

C H A P. XVII.
Of the Father and the Mother.

THe Lords of the fourth, and of the part of the Father,burnt out of their proper houſes and exaltations,ſignifie that the Father cannot long liue ; The ill fortunes within the 4. ſignifie that the father ſhall dye preſently after, if within the ſaid houſe they bee not dignified,or if the fortunes doo not enterlace their fauourable beames : Likewiſe you muſt iudge of the mother,when the ſayd Conſtellations ſhall be in the 10. The fortunes in the 4. ſignifie long life to the Father,and happie fortune :& likewiſe of the mother,when they be within the x. The Sunne vnfortunate within the iiij. or viij. houſe,teſtifieth that the Father ſhall not liue long : likewiſe you muſt iudge of the mother when the Moone ſhal
bee

bee ſo diſpoſed. If the Lord of the 4. be in the 11. the
childe ſhall ſee the death of his Father. If the Lord of the
x. be in the 5. he ſhall ſee the death of his mother. Venus
or the Moone in the 4. vnfortunate, giueth perrill to the
mother at her deliuerance.   The Lord of the 4. in the 7.
or 12. houſe, or in euill aſpects of ill fortunes , ſignifieth
ſtrife and quarrells betweene the Father and the Sonne.
Likewiſe you muſt iudge of the mother, when the Lord
of the 10. ſhall be in the ſame diſpoſition. The part of
the Father fortunate, denoteth long and happy life to the
Father : vnfortunate, he ſhall dye very quickly. The part
of the mother ſignifieth as much of the mother , after her
good or euill diſpoſition.

Commonly the Aſtrologians haue regard to the Sunne
and to Saturne for the Father, and to Venus and the
Moone for the mother ; If the natiuitie bee by day, they
take the Sun for ſignificator of the father : if it by be night
they take Saturne, if the Sunne be not in any angle of heauen : For if it be in the 1. or 4. they preferre him alwayes
to Saturne. If the Sunne be in the 1. in the natiuitie of the
1. childe, the figure of the natiuitie of the Father and of
the Sonne ſhall be both one. The ſignificator of the Father, ioyned to the Fortunes, or receiuing their amiable a-
ſpects , denote good fortune and long life to the Father :
the contrary you muſt vnderſtand when they be vnfortunate.

If the Lorde of the aſcendant , and the Lorde of the
4. doo looke with an euill aſpect , the Sonne and the Father ſhall be in diſcorde, principally if Mars intermeddle
with his pernicious beames. For the mother you muſt
looke principally to Venus, if the natiuitie be by day : or
to the Moone if it be by night ; And after their good and
euill diſpoſitions, you muſt iudge the good or contrary
fortune of the mother.

E 3   Of

CHAP. XVIII.
Of inheritances and earthly goods.

THE Fortunes, or other Plannets fortunate, within the fourth or eight house, denoteth inheritances and possessions : the ill fortunes doe deny or difpife them. Saturne, naturall significator of heritages, landes and poffefions, well difpofed, dooth giue great goods and landes, and maketh the man happie in labouring and tyllage ; That alfo fignifieth the fignificators of ryches, when they bee well difpofed within the houfes of Satuine. And the part of heritages, and the part of fortune in fowers & tyllers whē they be fortunate, with their Lords. If the fayde fignificator be vnfortunate, you muft iudge the contrary.

When one felfe Plannet is lorde of the firft and fourth houfe, the childe fhall haue inheritances which fhall enrich him, if the fayd lorde be fortunate : and if he fell and difpearfe them, he is vnfortunate. The lorde of the afcendant, or the Moone within the fourth fortunate, and amiably by Iupiter or Venus regarded, denote that he fhal finde fome great fumme of money vnder the earth, principally, if Saturne caft his Trynes or Sextil beames : or that of Mines of golde and filuer he fhall be made rich.

The tayle of the Dragon in the fourth, maketh him to fell & difpearfe his goods. That doth alfo the head of the Dragon, when fhe is in a figne earthly or watrifh : In ayrie fignes or fiery, fhe giueth great goods and landes.

CHAP. XIX.

Of Infantes.

THe Fortunes in the fift, giue the children : the vnfortunes denyes them. Except when they be in their proper houfe or exaltations, for then they giue euill children ; that which they doo alfo, when regarding the faide houfe, or the lord of the fame, with euill

euill aſpeĉts. If the Lord of the firſt be burned , he giueth the children abortiues,or which preſently after their
birth,dye. If the ſayde lorde be in the xij he ſhall ſee the
death of his children. If he bee in the vij. or xii. or if a
like Plannet bee Lorde of the v. vij. or xij , hee ſhall
haue ſutes and queſtions with his children. The lorde of
the aſcendlant , in euill aſpeĉt of the lorde of the v. denoteth as much. Before you giue iudgement of the Children, you muſt conſider the x. and the vii. houſe, and the
parts of children with their lordes. The ſignificators of
the children in Maſculine ſignes,ſignifieth Male children.
in feminines,denote daughters: Likewiſe you muſt iudge
when they bee coupled with plannets, maſeulines, or feminines.

C H A P. XX.

Of Seruaunts.

THe ſignifications of ſeruaunts muſt be taken of the
place of Mars & Mercurie, of the ſixt houſe of the
part of ſeruaunts,and of their lordes. The which
fortunate giueth faythfull ſeruauntes, vnfortunate
giue them euill. When the lord of the aſcendant & the
lord of the ſyxt ſhalbe in good aſpeĉt together to the ſyg-
nificators of riches, the child ſhalbe come rich by the in-
duſtrie and faythfulneſſe of his ſeruants. Likewiſe when
the fortunes be within the ſyxt houſe : to the contrarie,
when the Significator of riches ſhalbe vnfortunate in the
ſyxt houſe,he ſhall be vndone by his ſeruants. Likewiſe
when the ill fortunes ſhalbe in the ſaid houſe. If the lord
of the vi. be in the x. he ſhall yeelde his ſeruaunts more
greater maiſters then himſelfe. If the lord of the vi.houſe
be in the ſigne of a humane figure , his ſeruauntes ſhall
beare him reuerence and be at his commaundement.

E 4

The firſt Booke of

♄ *Fortunate.*

Sadde & of a deepe cogitation. Secrete. Solitarie. Laboursome. Painful. A heaper of goods. Patient. Sparing. Carefull of hys owne preferment.

♄ *Vnfortunate.*

An abiect. A fugitiue. Baſe minded. A vile man. Negligent. Fearefull. Sadde or penſiue. Couetous. Enuious. A Witch. Stubberne. A Roge. Suſpicious. Superſtitious. A Deceiuer.

♃ *Fortunate.*

A louer of GOD. Religious. Honeſt and vertuous. Stoute. Couragious. Iuſt. Vpright. Authoritie. Modeſtie. Bountifull.

♃ *Vnfortunate.*

A louer of hymſelfe. High-minded. Proude. Superſtitious. feareful. faint-harted. Careles or negligent. Prodigall. Nothing ſo good as when he is fortunate.

♂ *Fortunate.*

Gentle. Manly-minded. Full of courage. Stoute. Irefull. Earneſt. Fearing no danger. Patient. Delighting in warres and manly exerciſes.

♂ *Vnfortunate.*

Quarrelſome. Cruell. Angry. Tyranical. Vniuſt. Vnfaithfull. A blood-ſhedder. Theeuiſh. A make-bate. Haſtie, or raſhe. A boaſter. Very proude.

♀ *Fortunate.*

Pleaſant. Merry. Fayre. Gentle of ſpeech. Of comlie ieſture. Good. Mercifull. Gyuen to pleaſure both of bodie and minde. A louer of dainty and delicate thinges.

♀ *Vnfortunate.*

Womaniſh. Fearefull. Weake of nature. Slothful. Lecherus. A ſlaunderer. Not caring for his good name. Giuen to filthy luſt. Sodomiticall.

Fortunate.

☿ *Fortunate.*

Of an excellent wit, Studious. Of a quicke capasitie.
Of a good and founde iudgement in euery thing. Poeti-
call. Gramatical. Mathematical. Finding out many things
vntaught.

☿ *Unfortunate.*

Vnstable. Malicious. A lyer, chiefely if he be with the
Dragons tayle. Priuily sowing deceite. A slaunderer, For-
getful. Foolish. Full of wicked counsell and malice.

Thus may you gather the naturall disposition of anie
man, eyther present or absent: according to the nature of
the Planets as is aboue specified. As for the lyghtes, the
☽ from her ♂ to her ☍ dooth make theyr manners most
apparant, from her ☍ to her ♂ more obscure.

CHAP. XXI.

Of Diseases.

YOV must first of all consider the places of Saturne
and of Mars, and of the Lord of the sixt house. And
according to the signe in the which they bee, you
must iudge the sicknesse to bee in the place marked by the sayd signe. As if Saturne were in the signe of
Libra, it denoteth that the sicknes is in the reynes of the
nature of Saturne : becaufe that Libra is the signe that
hath gouernment ouer the reynes, as shall be declared in
the feconde Booke. Likewife you must iudge of other
Significators, after the gouernment of the signe in the
which they be.

The sicknes and accidents comming by Saturne, Mars
and other Planets, shalbe explaned in the fecond booke.
Mars in the afcendant, gyueth alwaies fome notable hurt
vpon the face, or vpon the head, and often neere the eyes,
when hee is neere the lights. Saturne in the first house,
yeeldeth the man to be very fadde, and melancholie, and
vexeth the minde, caufing horrible ill and fearefull ima-

F.   ginations.

ginations. The tayle of the Dragon in the first, darkeneth much the fight, and often yeeldes the men blind, when the Luminaries or the fortunes, doe not intermingle their fauourable beames. Saturne and Mars in the tenth, signifie sicknes in the necke, in the seauenth, in the buttockes: as Fistuloes, Emrods, Vlcers, and hurts. &c. In the sixt, diseases in the feete: in the twelfth, hurts and griefes in the legges, as I haue often tryed. Saturne infortunate, signifieth diseases in the parts appertaining to Saturne. Iupiter and the other, signifie as much when they be euill disposed. Of the partes which belong to the Planets wee will speake of in the second Booke.

They which haue the Lumynaries, or any of the principall places in the figure vnfortunate in the signe of Scorpio, are subiect to the French-pocks. The ill fortunes in the signe of Gemini, gyue alwaies some great and violent blowes vpon the shoulders, legges & armes. The Moone vnfortunate in the signe of Aries, signifieth great paine in the head. Saturne and Mars ioyned to the Lumynaries, or to the Lord of the ascendant, trouble the sight, and spoyle the eyes with some blowe. The Sunne in the natiuities Diurnes, signifyeth the right eye, the Moone the left: in the Nocturnes, to the contrary. If the degrees of the first house, or the Lumynaries be ioyned with any troublesome starre, the eyes shall be darke, and the sight troubled; lykewise if they be in the signes which the Astrologers call *Azemena* and filthy dregges. &c.

Saturne in the sixt house burned in a watry signe, denoteth some forme of leprosie. Saturne in the ascendant, maketh some notable deformitie in the face, when hee is neere the Moone. The ill fortunes, and the Moone and Venus in watry signes, signifie leprosie, vlcers & cankers on the body, and villainous spots in the face. Saturne in the ninth, and the Moone in the eyght vnfortunate, denote trouble of minde and folly. Venus ioyned to Mercurie vnfortunate by Saturne or Mars, without aspect of Iupiter or of the Sun, signifie notable griefe in the partes

of

of generation. If Venus & Mercury be vnder the beames of the Sunne, they signifie as much. Saturne wyth the Moone burned, causeth Palsies and Impostumes. Mercurie vnfortunate, gyueth alwaies some impediment in the tongue : and so doth Saturne also when he is vnfortunate in the temporall lights. The Sunne vnfortunate, denoteth weakenes of the hart : principally when he is lord of the sixt house, or Lord of the part of sicknesses. The ill fortunes with the tayle of the Dragon, cause loosenesse and the flixe of the bellie. They that haue the Sunne or Mars in the signes of Aries or Gemini, be subiect to the Stone. The retrogradation and burning of Saturne and Iupiter, spoyle the hearing, and the teeth.

When the Moone & Mercury doe not looke between them, and doe not regard the ascendant, nor the Lord of the ascendant, the chylde shall be troubled in his vnderstanding. The retrogradation of all the fiue Planets, signifyeth the falling sicknes. The ill fortunes ioyned in the ascendant in euill aspects of the Moone or the Lorde of the ascendant, denote entire folly. The part of sicknesses with hys Lord fortunate, preserueth from sicknes, vnfortunate, gyue many euils.

Chap. XXII.

Of Marriage.

FOR the marriage, you must looke the vij. house and hys Lord, the places of Venus and the Moone in the natiuities of men, and in the places of the Sunne and of Mars in natiuities of women : and the parts of marriage, and the place of Iupiter. If the sayde Significators be fortunate, the marriage shall be happie, if they be vnfortunate, it shall be full of enuies, reproches and euils. If some be fortunate, and some vnfortunate by certaine tymes, now happy, and then vnhappy, it shall be manifest. Many Planets in the seauenth house, giue many women : likewise when many Planets regard the say'd house or his Lord. If Venus,& the Lord of the seauenth house be burned,or otherwise of Saturne oppressed , the chylde shall neuer marry. Iupiter and Venus within the 6. or 8. signifyeth that he shall marry a widdow. Iupiter burned, signifieth as much. Otherwise, if Iupiter behold Venus , and the other significators of marriage, it promiseth maydes and virgins. If Venus or Iupiter, or the Lord of the seauenth house be ioyned to Saturne , or if Saturne be within the seauenth house, the woman shall haue some note of infamie; (that is to vnderstande) shee shall be of a strange religion,or shall be a bastard, or shall be of the race of Lepors, or of some other, by whom the Parents haue receiued some shame, or she shal be deformed, and her Parents shall be of a very weake condition. Mars in the sayd house, or beholding with euil aspect the Significators of marriage, intermingle strife and contentions betweene the man and the wife : the same doth also Venus in the seauenth or twelfth house.

Mars in the ninth, asmuch in the natiuities of women as of men, denoteth some manner of separation of marriage. And Venus in the ninth,signifieth that the man shal hate his wife, not so much for the vice which he shal find in her, but of a desire to be solitary. The Significators of marriage vnfortunate,or within the houses Cadents, signifieth the woman to be of a simple race, or the husbande in the natiuities of women.

If Venus and the Lorde of the seauenth house , ioyne with the Significators of riches,beholding the Lord of the ascendant with an amiable aspect, she giues much goods by reason of women. The Significators of mariage within the thyrd or ninth , or else where Peregrines, signifie that he shall marry out of hys Country . The fortunes within the seauenth house, denoteth happy marriage, the ill fortunes vnhappy. The Lorde of the seauenth within the seconde, denoteth that hee shall see the death of hys wife. The Significators of marriage occidentall, witnesse that he shall marry late, or in his youth take a wife older
then

then himfelfe. Orientall, denoteth that he fhall marrie in hys youth, or in hys age marry a young wife. Likewife you muft iudge of husbands in the natiuities of women.

Of a dowery and other goods by the meanes of marriage.

BIEcaufe the eyght houfe is fucceeding to the feauenth, by good reafon it fignifieth the profit of the fignifications of the feauenth, (that is to fay) of marriage. If then in the eyght there bee any fortunate Planet, or any part fortunate, the chyld fhall haue great dowrie by his wife, and of that fide fhall meet with great inheritaunces & great goods. To the contrary, if Saturne and Mars be vnfortunate in the faid houfe, hee fhall haue fmall dowery, and the fame fhall neuer be fully payd.

When the fortunes be in the fayd houfe vnfortunate, he hath hope of great goods the which in the end he fhal not enioy. The Lord of the faid place vnfortunate, denoteth as much: and if hee be fortunate and coupled with the Significators of riches, it denoteth great goods and great profite on that fide. It happeneth well fometimes when the feauenth houfe is fortunate, and the eyght vnfortunate. As that which fignifieth a little dowery & defperation of other goods towards his wife, & that alwaies he fhall be inriched by the diligence, induftry, and faithfulneffe of his wife.

Of the Death.

YOV muft firft confider if there bee any Planet in the eyght houfe, for it is conuenient to take it for Significator of the death. If within the fayde houfe there be neuer a Planet, take them for Significators that be in the feauenth, preferring him alwaies that is beft dignifyed. If within the feauenth you finde none, drawe

the

the Sgnifycator of the death from theſe places which followe.

Of the aſcendant and of his Lord.

Of the eyght houſe and of his Lord.

Of the part of Death and of his Lord.

Of the eyght Signe, from the place of the Sunne & of
hys Lorde.

Of the eyght Signe, from the Moone and of his Lord.

Of the place of the firſt Lorde of the triplicitie of the
fourth angle.

Of the place of the Planet which hath dignity of terme,
to the degree of the ſeauenth houſe.

The Planet which in all theſe places ſhall be moſt dignifyed, ſhall be principall Sgnificator of death.

If Saturne beeing in the eyght or ſeauenth houſe, or o-
therwiſe more dignified in the aboue ſaide poynts of the
figure, he is principall ſignificator of the death. If hee be
well diſpoſed, it witneſſeth, that the ſame partie ſhall dye
of the Dropſy, of ſome great ſtopping of the lyuer, and
of the Spleene, or of a quarterne Feuer, of the flixe of the
belly, of Pthiſick, or of ſome burning Feuer, and of Impoſtumations of the eares. &c. If it be greatly vnfortunate,
and together with the Lord of the aſcendant, and the luminaries temporally be euill diſpoſed, it denoteth violent
death by Impoſtumes, Palſies, falling downe of humors,
ſuffocations, ouer-flowen with water. When it is in watry Signes, by ſome fall or ruine : when it is in earthlie
Signes, by great blowes : for to be hanged when it is in
ayerie Signes.

If Iupiter be Significator of the death, it denoteth that
he ſhall die of a Plureſie, of a Squinance, or of ſome hote
appoſtumations of the lyuer, or of the lunges, or of other
ſickneſſes comming of wind or of blood ; and that if he be
fortunate. For when he is euill diſpoſed and vnfortunate,
it maketh hym die by the hand of iuſtice, by the commandement of the Prince, by ſentence of the Iudge or of the
Marſhall, by ouer-flowing in waters, to be whypped and

ſcourfcourged, by long imprifonment.

If it be *Mars* well difpofed, by continuall tertian Feuers, by flixe of blood, by Carbuncles and peftilences, by Impoftumes comming of chollerick matters, burnings by too much vfing of women. If he be very euil difpofed, it maketh him to be hanged and ftrangled, or fmothered, or otherwife killed in his bedde, or on hys horfe. When he is an ayrie figne or partaker within the water, when he is a watry figne or fallen frō on high, or of fome ruinous murtherer. When he is a terreftiall, or burned: when he is a fierie Signe: principally if the Lord of the afcendant and the luminaries temporally be vnfortunate by Mars. If it be the Sunne well difpofed, hee fhall die of fome hote difeafe. If it be vnfortunate, by the commaundement of the Prince, or by fentence of the Iudge, or hee fhall dye among a great company of men, fubiect to death, or in prifon, or in a Dungeon, or in fome other ftincking and filthy place. If it be Venus wel difpofed, he fhal die of too much eating fruites, or with too much continuing his voluptuoufnes, or of fome Fiftula or Impoftume. If fhe be vnfortunate, it denoteth death by venim, principallie when fhe is burned, or ioyned to Saturne, or of too much burning affection of loue, or of great griefes of the French pockes. If it be Mercurie fortunate, it maketh him dye by fadneffe, by great apprehenfions, by the Yellowe iaunders, by pthifickes, by the burning Feuer, or by too much watching. If he be greatly vnfortunate, it fignifieth that he fhall die by madneffe, the Falling-ficknes, by violent Coughes, with breaking in funder the veynes, by foolifh mellancholie, by Ieloufie.

If it be the Moone well difpofed, with too much eating moyft meates, by drinking water, by too much continuing his pleafure; If fhe be vnfortunate, you muft confider the nature of him which is vnfortunate. For if it be Mars hee fhall dye by fire, or by hurt: or by abortifment if it be a woman. If it bee Saturne, by ruines, falles, peftilences, and like accidents.

Before

the Sgnifycator of the death from theſe places which folⵏ
lowe.

Of the aſcendant and of his Lord.

Of the eyght houſe and of his Lord.

Of the part of Death and of his Lord.

Of the eyght Signe, from the place of the Sunne & of hys Lorde.

Of the eyght Signe, from the *Moone* and of his Lord.

Of the place of the firſt Lorde of the triplicitie of the fourth angle.

Of the place of the Planet which hath dignity of terme, to the degree of the ſeauenth houſe.

The Planet which in all theſe places ſhall be moſt dignifyed, ſhall be principall Sgnificator of death.

If Saturne beeing in the eyght or ſeauenth houſe, or otherwiſe more dignified in the aboue ſaide poynts of the figure, he is principall ſignificator of the death. If hee be well diſpoſed, it witneſſeth, that the ſame partie ſhall dye of the Dropſy, of ſome great ſtopping of the lyuer, and of the Spleene, or of a quarterne Feuer, of the flixe of the belly, of Pthiſick, or of ſome burning Feuer, and of Impoſtumations of the eares. &c. If it be greatly vnfortunate, and together with the Lord of the aſcendant, and the luminaries temporally be euill diſpoſed, it denoteth violent death by Impoſtumes, Palſies, falling downe of humors, ſuffocations, ouer-flowen with water. When it is in watry Signes, by ſome fall or ruine : when it is in earthlie Signes, by great blowes : for to be hanged when it is in ayerie Signes.

If Iupiter be Significator of the death, it denoteth that he ſhall die of a Plureſie, of a Squinance, or of ſome hote appoſtumations of the lyuer, or of the lunges, or of other ſickneſſes comming of wind or of blood ; and that if he be fortunate. For when he is euill diſpoſed and vnfortunate, it maketh hym die by the hand of iuſtice, by the commandement of the Prince, by ſentence of the Iudge or of the *Mar*ſhall, by ouer-flowing in waters, to be whypped and

ſcour-

scourged, by long imprisonment.

If it be *Mars* well disposed, by continuall tertian Feuers, by flixe of blood, by Carbuncles and pestilences,by Impostumes comming of chollerick matters, burnings by too much vsing of women. If he be very euil disposed, it maketh him to be hanged and strangled,or smothered, or otherwise killed in his bedde, or on hys horse . When he is an ayrie signe or partaker within the water, when he is a watry signe or fallen frō on high, or of some ruinous murtherer. When he is a terrestiall,or burned : when he is a fierie Signe : principally if the Lord of the ascendant and the luminaries temporally be vnfortunate by Mars.If it be the Sunne well disposed, hee shall die of some hote disease. If it be vnfortunate, by the commaundement of the Prince, or by sentence of the Iudge, or hee shall dye among a great company of men , subiect to death, or in prison, or in a Dungeon, or in some other stincking and filthy place.If it be Venus wel disposed,he shal die of too much eating fruites, or with too much continuing his voluptuousnes, or of some Fistula or Impostume. If she be vnfortunate, it denoteth death by venim , principallie when she is burned, or ioyned to Saturne,or of too much burning affection of loue,or of great griefes of the French pockes. If it be Mercurie fortunate, it maketh him dye by sadnesse, by great apprehensions , by the Yellowe iaunders, by pthisickes, by the burning Feuer,or by too much watching. If he be greatly vnfortunate, it signifieth that he shall die by madnesse, the Falling-sicknes, by violent Coughes,with breaking irrsunder the veynes, by foolish mellancholie, by Ielousie.

If it be the Moone well disposed,with too much eating moyst meates,by drinking water,by too much continuing his pleasure; If she be vnfortunate,you must consider the nature of him which is vnfortunate. For if it be Mars hee shall dye by fire , or by hurt : or by abortisment if it be a woman. If it bee Saturne, by ruines, falles, pestilences, and like accidents.

Before

Before concluding of what death the partie ſhall dye, you muſt conſider the diſpoſition of the Lorde of the aſcendant, and of the luminaries temporall: For if they be well diſpoſed, the death ſhal not be vyolent, although the principall ſignificator bee greatly vnfortunate, If the ſayd ſignificator be vnfortunate, together with the luminaries temporall, or the Lord of the aſcendant euill diſpoſed, we eſteeme certainly that the death ſhall be vyolent, if Iupiter or Venus doo not intermingle theyr fauourable beames, and then the ſayd perſon ſhall fall in great daunger of the ſaid violent death, & from the which he ſhall alwayes eſcape myraculoufly.

If one of the ill fortunes be in the ſigne of Cancer, and the other in the ſigne of the Lyon, the death ſhall be vyolent; Likewiſe, if any of the ſayde ill fortunes be in the ſigne of the Lyon, and the luminaries temporall, or the Lord of the aſcendant be vnfortunate, and one of the ill fortunes be in the firſt houſe, and the other in the ſeuenth or fourth, or one of them in the tenth and the other in the fourth.

The Sunne, or the Moone, or the Lord of the aſcendant, ioyned with Mars, haue right in one fixed ſtarre, which the Aſtrologers cal the head of Meduſe, or otherwiſe the head of the diuel, maketh him by the hand of the Executioner to leeſe his head.

When the Sunne, and the Moone, and Saturne, and Mars, occupie the 4. angles of heauen, or at the leaſt 3. the perſonne ſhall dye a horrible death: for he ſhall leeſe his head, or be cut in foure.quarters, or be drawen with foure horſes: principally, if in the ſayde angles be the ſignes of Gemini, Piſces and Aquarius. Mars in the ninth or eyght in the ſigne of Aquarius or of Gemini, oppoſite to the Moone, or the Lorde of the aſcendant, without good aſpect of fortunes, maketh hym perriſh by Sulpher or fire from heauen. Saturne in the twelfth, ſixt, eyght, or fourth houſe vnfortunate, the lord of the ſayde houſes maketh hym dye in pryſon, or els where in great payne

and

and trauaile : principally when the luminaries temporall, or the Lord of the ascendant be vnfortunate in any of the sayd houses.

The tayle of the Dragon beeing ioyned to the Significators of death, denote poysons, venims, and violent medicines, or ill applyed, and flixe of the belly. Mars within the fourth, eyght, twelfth, or sixt vnfortunate, theyr lords and the luminaries temporall, or the Lorde of the ascendant, witnesse violent death, by the shedding of blood or otherwise.

The Significators of death within the ninth or thyrd house, signifie that the person shall die by the way, or in a strange Country : except they be in theyr owne proper houses or exaltations, for then he shall die in his house, & bring his euill from the high waies. The said Significators in their proper houses or exaltations, make him die in his house, if they be Peregrines, they make him dye out of his house.

The Moone ioyned to a fixed starre, named the Claire of the ballance meridionall, denoteth violent death. That dooth she also when she is ioyned with other starres that haue the nature of the luminaries. Mars in the viij. house with the head of the Dragon, maketh him to bee hanged and strangled. Many Planets within the seauenth house, make him dye of some strange and terrible kind of death. Saturne, Mars, and the heade of the Dragon in the first, Venus and Mercurie with the taile in the seauenth, make the body in a thousand peeces.

If the principall Significator bee burned in his owne proper house or exaltation, without being otherwise vnfortunate, it maketh him dye suddainly of some feeblenes, or other suddaine and secrete accident, without other violence. The fortunes well disposed in the eyght house, preserue him alwaies from violent death.

G.   Of

Chap. XXV.
Of voyages by Land and by Sea.

I Vpiter, Venus, the Sunne and Mercurie fortunate in the ninth houſe, denote that he ſhall be happy in viages by Land and by Sea. Saturne and Mars ſignifie to the contrary; and principally Saturne doth hinder the viages by water, and Mars the waies by Lande. If within the ninth houſe there be neuer a Planet, you muſt conſider the Moone, and the Lord of the ninth, and the parts of the waies and viages by land and by water, with their Lordes, the which fortunate, giueth profitable nauigations: vnfortunate, denote the contrary. Likewiſe you muſt iudge of the third houſe and of his lord, when they be well or euill diſpoſed. The head of the Dragon in the ninth, fauoureth greatlie to the fortune of viages, and the tayle to the contrary.

Chap. XXVI.
Of the conſtancie in his Religion.

A Lſo as the head of the Dragon, the luminaries, and Mercurie in the ninth houſe well diſpoſed, denote entire fayth and conſtancie in hys Religion, Saturne, Mars, and the tayle of the Dragon do hynder it. Saturne of his nature is moſt enclined to the Law of the Iewes: and Mars to the law of the Turkes & Mahometiſts; the tayle of the Dragon, cauſeth him alwaies to erre from the truth of the law. The lord of the nynth, and the part of the fayth, with hys Dominator fortunate, yeeldeth a man conſtant in his faith: vnfortunate maketh him variable.

If the part of the ſpirite be in the ſigne of the Lyon at the byrth of a Chriſtian, hee ſhall be very conſtant in hys religion, if the Sunne be fortunate: if he be vnfortunate by Saturne, to goe from his fayth, and to addreſſe it to that of the Iewes. If he be vnfortunate by Mars, it maketh

keth him more to encline to the lawe of the Turkes and
Mahometifts. If the said part be in the houfes of Saturne
at the natiuitie of a Iewe, or in the houfes of Mars at the
natiuitie of a Turke, they fhall denie theyr lawe : if the
fayd lords of the fayd part be retrogrades, or otherwife ill
difpofed. Saturne in the nynth at the natiuitie of a Iewe,
doth nothing diminifh his faith. Saturne in the faid houfe
when he is fortunate, fignifieth Dreames to be true, Mars
and the tayle of the Dragon fignifie them vaine and falfe,
The other fignificators doe affure them to be true.

Chap. XXVII.
Of the action and profefsion.

HOW to knowe of what profefsion the childe fhall
be, you muft chiefely confider if any Planet be in
the tenth houfe, for he fhal be Significator of the
profefsion : otherwife, you muft come to the part
of Fortune, and to his lord, to the part of the profeffion,
and to his lord, to the tenth houfe, and to his lord, and to
the places of *Mars, Mercurie* and *Venus.*

The Planet that vpon thefe places fhal haue the moft
dignities, fhalbe Significator of the profeffion. The which
if it be Saturne, it fhall fignifie a Husbandman , a good
houfe-keeper, a Receiuer of rents, and many times a Go-
uernour of Townes, when he is in angles fortunate. Iupiter denoteth the officers, Iudges, Benefices, Prelates, By-
fhops, Gouernours of the goods of the Church. Mars fignifieth Captaines, men of warre, Coyners , Forgeours,
and other that vfe to worke with fire and yron : and Phi-
fitions when he is in the afpect of Venus.

Sol reprefenteth Princes, Lords, Magiftrates, Hunters, Treafurers and Archers. Venus Players, Dauncers,
Perfumers, Appothecaries, and in afpect of Mars, Phifi-
tions. Mercurie, Aduocates, Notaries, Regifters, Poets,
Rymers, Phylofophers, Mathematicians, Diuiners, wry-
ters, Meffengers and traders.

The

The Moone, Embaſſadors, Counſellers, Conſuls, Rulers of Common wealth, Trauailers, Hunters. If there be
many Significators, or if the principall bee coupled with
many Planers, you muſt mingle the ſignifications of the
one and of the other, and of the ſaid mixture, gather together the profeſsion comming of the concurrence of the
ſtarres. You muſt alſo conſider in what houſe the ſayde
Significators be, if they be within the ſecond, the profeſſion ſhall be of feates of merchandize and traffiques : if
within the third or ninth, of feates of religion, or gathering
the goods of the Church. If in angles, of Dominations &
gouernments. If in the fift of Embaſſages, legations, and
other things of pleaſure. If in the ſixt, of feates of diſeaſes,
of ſeruaunts and of Cattell. &c. If the part of the honour
comming of the profeſsion, be with his Lord fortunate, the
Infant ſhall obtayne great credite and honour becauſe of
his profeſsion. If they be vnfortunate, if hee doe neuer ſo
well, he ſhall neuer gayne to himſelfe honor in the feates
of his profeſsion.

Chap. XXVIII.
Of dignities, offices, and honours.

FOR the dignities, offices, charges and honors, you
muſt haue reſpect to the tenth houſe, to the luminaries temporall, to the part of noblenes, to the part
of gouernment, to the part of Magiſtrates, & others
appertaining to the tenth houſe, with theyr Lordes. The
Planet that in the ſayde places ſhall haue moſt dignities,
ſhall be Significator of the ſayd conſiderations in good or
euill, according to his good or euill diſpoſition : particulerly alſo you muſt follow the ſayde places one after another, to know of what ſide principally the ſayde dignities,
offices and honours ought to come.

Saturne in the tenth houſe, or in the aſcendant in natiuities by day, ſignifieth great aduauncement and honour
after thirty yeeres, when he is not euill diſpoſed : in natiuities

uities by night, it denoteth continuall feare,to receiue damage of Princes and Kings.   Mars in the fayde places in
natiuities by night, fignifieth alfo great aduauncement, &
by day more then Saturne.

The part of gouernment and his Lorde within any of
the angles, witnes great fauour of Kings. Likewife you
muft iudge of the other part that we haue deducted vpon
the tenth houfe. Mercurie in the tenth weil difpofed and
fortunate, promifeth dignities, offices and honours , by
reafon of knowledge. Venus and the Moone becaufe of
women. Iupiter for hys vertue. The Sunne and the head
of the Dragon in the fame houfe, denoteth as much. The
two luminaries in theyr houfes or exaltations placed in
the figure of Heauen, doe denote great aduauncement &
honour.

That which Iupiter dooth alfo when hee receiueth
the vertue of all the other Planets, & communicateth hys
owne to Saturne and the Sunne; and the fortunes and the
luminaries when they be in the angles of Heauen. Manie
Planets in the fourth houfe, denoteth great honour after
death. If in the poynts of the angles be any fixed ftarre of
the firft or fecond greatnes,or other hauing the nature of
lumynaries, it is a great figne of incredible aduancement.
That which happeneth alfo when the fayd ftarres be ioyned to the lumynaries temporall, or to the parte of Fortune,or to his Lord, or to the Planets and parts that bee
in the angles.

They which haue Saturne in the tenth burnt, or the
Lord of the tenth burnt, or be by Saturne oppreffed, or
that haue the tayle of the Dragon in the tenth , receiue
commonly fome forme of difhonour, and often be depriued of theyr eftate , vvhen the Fortunes doe not intermingle theyr fauourable beames : except when they be
alfo vnfortunate in theyr proper houfes or exaltations, or
in the fignes of Aries and the Lyon.

You muft note that Saturne & Mars,hinder greatly the
good fortunes,vntil that the man hath paffed the number

of yeres corriſpondent to the number of the ſmal yeres of the ſaid Planets : and if they hinder any more time, it ſhal bee vntill that the man ſhall accompliſh the number of yeeres aunſwering to the number of degrees, of the ouerthwart aſcentions of the Signe, in the which they ſhall be at the natiuity.

Chap. XXIX.
Of companions and Friendes.

YOV muſt for the Companions and Friendes, haue reſpect to Iupiter, the eleuenth houſe, the parte of friendes, the part of honourable companions. The Planet hauing moſt dignities in the ſaid places, ſhal be principall Significator of friends : the which after hys good or euill diſpoſition, ſhall denote honourable, faythfull, and profitable friendes : or vnprofitable, diſloyal, and of baſe condition. Iupiter and the Sunne in the ſaid houſe, ſignifie honourable companies and profitable : ſo dooth Venus, the Moone and Mercurie alſo in the ſaide place. Saturne in the eleuenth fortunat, witneſſeth graue friends, auncient and honourable. Mars, men of warre, Captaines and Lords.

Saturne or Mars in the eleuenth out of their principal dignities, depriued of the beames of the fauourable Planets, ſignifie ſome great ſute againſt hys friendes, or ſome great euill by reaſon of them : as it happeneth commonly to the Aunſwerers and Suerties. The parts of honorable companions and of praiſe, with theyr Lords fortunate, ſignifyeth profite and honour on the ſide of friendes : vnfortunate denoteth the contrary. The part of friendes denoteth as much.

The heade of the Dragon in the eleuenth houſe, gyueth fauour of friendes : the tayle denoteth a thouſande miſchiefes by reaſon of them.

Chap. XXX.
Of sutes and Enemies.

THE fortunes in the seauenth and twelfth house, gyue victories against enemies, when they bee in good aspect to the lord of the ascendant. And cōmonly those which haue these 2. houses with theyr Lordes fortunate, be happy in theyr sutes : the contrarie you must iudge, when they with theyr Lordes be vnfortunate. The ill fortunes in the sayde places, signifie much strifes and enemies. That doth also the parts of enemies, and of discord and accord, when they and theyr Lords be euill disposed.

The Lord of the twelfth house fortunate, it denoteth little puissaunce of enemies : vnfortunate denoteth the contrary. If one of the two ill fortunes be in the twelfe, and the other in the sixt, in euill aspect of the lumynaries temporall, or of the Lord of the ascendant, the chylde shall be killed by his enemies. They which haue Saturne, or Mars, or the Moone opposite to the Sun in the Signe of Cancer, be commonly contrary to all the world. Mars in any of the foure angles, ingendereth naturally stryfe, sutes, debates, and enmities against all the world: except when he is in a good aspect of Iupiter and Venus. For then he doth expell hys ire and anger against the vices, & of great zeale maintaineth the right of euery one.

The Lorde of the ascendant, or the Moone, or the Sunne vnfortunate in the twelfe house, denoteth great persecutions and calamities of the enemies. The Lord of the ascendant by the lord of the twelfe oppressed, testifieth that he shall die by the hand of his enemies.

The Lord of the twelfe, and the Planets that be in the seauenth & twelfe house, signifie the qualitie of enimies, (that is to vnderstand) the Sunne signifieth the Princes & great Lords, the Moone all the world, and Mars the men of warre. &c.

Of

CHAP. XXXI.

Of imprisonments and c. priuities.

THE Lord of the ascendant, or the Moone or the Sunne greatlie vnfortunate in the 12. 6. 8. and 4. house, doe signifie imprisonments, and death within the prysons, or in captiuitie : principally when they be burned out of theyr principall dignities, and out of the signes of Aries and the Lyon, and when they bee oppressed by Saturne lorde of one of the sayd houses. Saturne and Mars in the angles of Heauen, signifie alwaies some imprisonment : and principally Saturne. Mercurie in the angles vnder the beames of the Sunne, receiuing an euill aspect of ill fortunes, signifieth as much. If Mercurie or the lorde of the ascendant gyue his vertue to Saturne, beeing in the eyght house , it signifieth that the chylde shall dwell long in prison and captiuity.

If the lord of the ascendant bee in the twelfe in a signe of a humane figure, without aspects of fortunes or of luminaries, hee shall be captiue and a slaue in his youth. If the lorde of the nynth be burned in any of the angles of Heauen, he shall be taken by the high-waies, and put in pryson.

The parts of prison, and of paine, trauayle and affliction with theyr lords burnt, or otherwise vnfortunate, signifieth imprisonment and captiuitie . That dooth also the vnfortunes when they bee well dignified in the sayde places.

The partes of all enuies , and of the perrillous yeere doth signifie as much, when they with theyr Lordes bee greatly vnfortunate.

The sayde parts with theyr Lords fortunate, preferueth from prison, and from captiuitie.

Of

CHAP. XXXII.
Of Horses, Sheepe, and other beastes.

THE fortunes and Planets fortunate within the 6. and twelfe house, yeelde the men happy in horses and nourishing of beastes. The lords of the sayde houses fortunate, and coupled with the Significators of riches, signifie as much. Naturally the sixt house denoteth Sheepe, and Goates, and other small beastes, the 12. Horses, Oxen, Kine, Camels, & other great beastes. The ill fortunes within the sayd houses, or the lordes of the sayd houses vnfortunate, signifie losse and damage of the said beastes.

Saturne and *Mars* in the twelfe, maketh the horses to fall with notable losse. The which they doe also whē they be elswhere in the Signe of Sagitarius. The lorde of the natiuitie in the twelfe house in euill aspect of the Lord of the twelfe, maketh hym fall from his horse in great perrill of death, when the fortunes & luminaries do not yeeld theyr amiable aspects.

If the twelfe be of Sagittarius or the Lyon, & the lord of the ascendant, or the Sunne, or the *Moone* be vnfortunate, hee shall fall from hys horse and dye, if the fortunes within the eyght house doe not hinder the euill.

The end of the first Booke.

H.   Of

The second Booke of

Of the Aſtronomical iudgements
vpon the Natiuities, contayning particuler conſiderations.

The ſecond Booke.

CHAP. I.
Of the ſignifications of the Planets.

SAturne, hauing regard ouer the right part of Septentrion, ouer the earth and the water, ouer the melancholie, and ſometimes ouer the phlegme, groſſe
humors, ouer the eares, the ſpleene, the bladder, the
mawe, the ſinowes, and the bones. And ſignifieth pale
men, or black, leane, penſiue, ſolitarie, fearefull, raylers,
graue, contemplators, labourers, Maſons, buyers of rents,
Vſurers, Carpenters, Fiſhers, Merchants of oyles, Leather, Fiſh, tyles, ſtone, allome. &c. Of diſeaſes it ſignifieth
leperouſnes, cankers, rottennes, quarterne-feuers, opilati-
ons, dropſies, flixe of the belly, collicke, burſtneſſe in the
coddes, miſconception of women, the gowte in the legs,
gowte in the wriſtes, Sciatiqua, deafenes, the falling ſicknes, fooliſh melancholy, very difficult in fetching breath,
& others, ingendered of groſſe humors or of wind, which
endure long. Of ages, oldnes: of partes of the yeere Autumne: of colours the black, cleer, tawny, dark: of ſauors,
the ſharpe and abſtringent, pricking with ſharpnes: of
dayes, the Saturday: of Regions, Bauieres, Saxony, Ro-
manie, Conſtance, and the firſt Clymate. Of particuler
places, Caues, Lakes, Pondes, cloſe places, olde & ruinous
houſes, ſolitary places, obſcure deſerts & ſtinking places.

Iupiter

Iupiter regarding the occident,the ayre,the blood with the vitall ſpyrits, the lunges, the ſides , the lyuer and the veynes: and ſignifieth men of good ſtature,and ful faced, bald,curled, white with a pleaſant redneſſe intermingled, hauing the eyes indifferent great, the noſtrils reaſonable ſhort, the fore-teeth reaſonable great, honeſt men, gratious, bleſſed, religious, Abbots, Byſhops , Prelates, Officers, Iudges, Magiſtrates. With copulation of Saturne, it ſignifieth Nigromancers, Enchaunters, Sorcerers. With Mars, Phiſitions. With the Sunne, appeaſors of quarrels, controuerſies and diſputations. With Venus,Muſitions. With Mercurie, Mathematicians. With the Moone, Geometricians, Geographers,& Hidrografers. Of Diſeaſes, it ſignifieth burning Feuers,Quincies,Pluriſies,ſwellings, Impoſtumes, phlegmes, and other, comming of bloode. Of ages, betweene age and youth. Of the partes of the yeere, the Spring-time.

Of colours, as cleere as a Saphire, as yellowe as a Citterne, greene,and a lyttle drawing vpon the redde. Of fauours ſweete and amiable. Of dayes , the Thurſday. Of Countries, Babylon, Perſia, Hungarie, Spayne,and the ſecond Clymate. Of particuler places, churches, pallaces, priuiledged places, cleane,honeſt,and religious.

Mars looking towards the South, the fire,cholléricke humors, the reynes, the payne in the noſtrils, the gaule, the genitories. He denoteth men with red faces, and the ſkinne redde, the face round, the eyes yellow, horrible to behold,furious men, cruell, deſperate, proude, ſedicious, ſouldiers, Captaines, Smythes, Colliers, Bakers, Alcumiſtes, Armourers, Furniſhers, Butchers, Chirurgions, Barbers, Sargiants and Hangmen, according as they ſhal be well or euill diſpoſed.

With Saturne , commonly it ſignifieth Chirurgions. With Iupiter, Naturall Philoſophers & Phyſitions.With the Sunne, healers of eyes. VVith Venus , Barbers and Sheremen. With Mercury,men of skil to let blood. With the Moone, Tooth-drawers,and clenſers of the eares. Of
diſeaſes,

diseases,it denoteth tertian Feuers, and continuall impediments, pestilences, megrams of the head, carbunckles, ring-wormes, blisters, chollericks and burnings, madnes, phrensies, issues of blood, vomiting of blood, chollericke pasions, the yellow Iaunders, the bloody-fluxe,& others, comming of chollericke humors and burnings. Of ages, the flower of youth. Of the parts of the yeere , the Sommer.

Of colours, red, flame-colour, sanguine, and drawing to an yron colour. Of sauours, the bitter and sharpe. Of Of the dayes, Tuesday. Of Regions, Getulie, Lombardie, and the third Clymate. Of places particuler, houses of Smythes, Coyners of money, slaughters, furnices , all places dedicated to fyer, yron and blood.

The Sunne hauing domination ouer the East & South, ouer the fire,ouer the pure blood,and ouer the vital spyrites, ouer the eyes, ouer the brayne, ouer the hart. And it signifieth wisemen,prudent, dyscreete, couetous of glorie and of honour : of an indifferent stature, browne of colour,great bearded,yellow eyed,the face marked,a great voyce, and very ill fauoured. Honourable men, Officers, Magistrates, Lords, Princes, Kings and Gouernours of Countries and great hunters.And with Saturne,denoteth principall Meaters, Rentets, and labourers honourable. With Iupiter, Beneficed men, Pryors, Abbots, and Prelates,or Iudges and Officers of iustice. With Mars,Captaines and Conductors of warres. With Venus , Gouernours of the goods of Princes , and officers of the same. With Mercurie, Counsellers, Secretaries, Chauncellors. With the Moone, Legates, Embassadours, and honourable messengers.

Of diseases, hote rumes vpon the face, and vppon the eyes, rednes of the face, tympanies , palpitation of the hart, dolor of the heade comming of too much bloode,or with tarrying long in the beames of the Sunne. Of ages, youth. The parts of the yeere, the beginning of Sommer. Of colours the yellow, the cleere redde, colour of golde.

Of

Of fauours, fowernes and fweetneſſe agreeably inter-mingled. Of dayes, Sunday. Of Countries, Italy, Cicilha, Bohemia, and the fourth Clymate. Of particuler places, houſes of Princes, Pallaces, Theaters, and other large places, excellent and cleere.

Venus Dominatrix ouer the right parte of the Eaſt, vpon the ayre and water, vppon the mixtion of phlegme, blood and ſpyrits, and feede of generation. Vppon the reynes, belly, nauill, lyuer, backe, and other partes dedi-cated to generation. And ſignifieth white men or browne, with ſome redneſſe intermingled: fayre faced, pleaſant lookes, hawke-nofed, full of hayre, ioyfull, laughter, libe-rall, pleaſers, dauncers, entertayners of women, players, perfumers, muſitions, meſſengers of loue. With Saturne, it ſignifieth Preachers, and others that ſing and ioyfullie aſſiſt at deceafes and burials. With Iupiter, muſitians and others, which ſing the prayſe of God in folemne hymnes. With Mars, trumpeters and dromſlades in warre. Wyth Mercurie, ſingers of rymes & poetry. With the Moone, ſingers of common ſongs. Of difeaſes, impoſtumes, and of moyſt matters, fyſtuloes, imbecility of the ſtomach, of the reynes, and of the part of generation, folly comming by too much loue, the French-pockes with his ſuppor-ters, and other, comming of cold and moyſt matter, and of veniims.

Of ages, young yeeres: of parts of the yeere, the be-ginning of the Spring-time: of colours, the white, greene, redde, and a little yellow; of fauours, the fweete, deleɕta-ble, and ſauourlieſt. Of dayes, Friday: of Regions, Ara-bia, Auſtria, Sweecherland, and the fift Clymate. Of par-ticuler places, neere gardens, fountaynes, Chambers well decked, halles hanged with Tapeſtry, beds wel adorned, and others, dedicated to playes, dauncies, ſongs and al vo-luptuoufneſſe.

Mercurie beeing chiefe ouer the Septentrion ouer the water and earth, and of the ſpyrits of beaſtes, and ouer the confuſion of humors. Ouer the hands, feete, armes, ſhoul-

ders,

ders, tongue, mouth and teeth. And fignifieth men ney-
ther white nor blacke : leane : of fmal ftature : long finge-
red : long faced : high fore-headed : the nofe ftraight and
long : little beard : full of hayre : the eyes little & quicke :
fubtile men : ingenious : vnconftant : Rymers : Poets :
Aduocates : Orators : Phylofophers : Sooth-fayers : A-
rithmeticians : Merchants : and bufie fellowes.

With Saturne, Geomitricians : Architects : With Iupiter, Lawyers : Cannons : and thofe that keepe the Regifters of the benefits of Churches and futes. With Mars,
Sargiants of the bande, Archers of the Garde. &c. With
the Sunne, Maifters of the houfes of Princes and great
Lords : and theyr Secretaries & Stewards. With Venus,
Mufitions : Apothicaries and Perfumers. The Moone,
trauailers, meffengers & traffiquers. Of difeafes, vertigo
or turning of the head : lightnes of the braine : like to follie : foolifh imaginations : lets of the tongue : pthifickes :
iffues in the legges, feete and hands : and other, that haue
caufes hydden, and that come by certaine times. Of ages,
the time betweene feauen and fourteene yeeres : Of the
parts of the yeere, Autumne. Of colours, the ftrangeft, di-
uerft and mixtious. Of fauours, the ftrangeft & of newe
taft. Of dayes, Wednefday. Of Countries, Egipt, Greece,
England, Flaunders : Paris : and the 6. Clymate. Of particuler places, fhops : fayers : comon-markets : fchooles :
halles of Lawyers.

The Moone doth gouerne ouer the right part of the
Weft : ouer the water : ouer the phlegme : fweatinges :
monthly flowers : and like fuperfluities. Ouer the ftomacke : the belly : the brayne : the lunges : the breft and
the eyes. And fignifieth men of fayre ftature, white, and
the face round and fpotted : the eyes a little blacke, and a
little lowring : long bearded : hys eye-browes knit together : amiable men, peaceable : Trauailers : Pilgrims :
Hunters : Embaffadors : Legates : Confuls : Atturneyes :
Benchers : Gouernours of Townes : principall in deedes
of pollicie.

With Saturne, it fignifieth Carters and vile Workers.
With Iupiter, Geomitricians and Geographers. Wyth
Mars, Drawers of teeth : Alcumifts and Blowers. With
the Sunne, honourable meffengers. With Venus, carriers
of packs. With Mercury, Poets, Rymers, meffengers, trauailers and traffiquers. Of difeafes, gowtes of the feete
& wriftes : fciatiqua: dropfies: lyttargy : palfies : rumes:
fhaking of the members: drowfie fickneffes : flixe of the
bellie : vomitings : fiftuloes : wormes : and other caufes
of cold and moyftnes. Of ages, the infancie : of the partes
of the yeere, Winter : of colours, white : yellow : greene :
of fauours, the faltifh : frefh : or without fauour : of daies,
Monday. Of Countries, Flaunders : Affrick : and the feauenth Clymate. Of particuler places, fieldes : fountaines :
mountaines : Hauens of the Sea : woods : high-waies and
defert places.

Chap. II.
¶ Of the fignifications of the twelue Signes.

ARies doth gouerne ouer the hart of the Orient, o-
uer the fire, ouer the chollerique humors & hote :
ouer the beginning of the Spring : ouer the head :
the nofe, the face, the eares and the eyes. And fignifieth leane men, redde coloured, flat nofed, chollericke,
ftrong, and right men of warre : Captaines : fouldiours :
Alcumiftes, and other martialifts. Of difeafes, it denoteth
lytargy : madneffe : iffues of bloode : rednes of the face :
filthineffe : falles : hurts : and all fickneffes violent and
continuall.

Of colours, redde : yellowe : and fanguine colour :
Of fauours, the fweete. Of Countries, Brittany : Alma-
nie : Inde : Iuda : England : Naples : Florence : Fauence :
Imole : Capne : Ferrara : Venice : Verone : Pauie : Cra-
conie : Marfelle : Saragoffe : and the third Clymate.

Of

Of particular places, feildes, pastures, houses of Forgiours of money, and places of blood, and iustice.

Taurus gouerneth ouer the left parte of the meridies, ouer the earth, ouer the melancholy humours, ouer the middle of the springe, ouer the necke, and throate. And signifieth little men, well fleshed with great shoulders, great eyes, large bellyed, paynefull men, liberall, trustie, voluptuous, messengers of loue, dauncers, players. Of sicknesses, the kings euill, Caterches, Squinacies, and other sicknesses of the necke. Of Coloure, the greene and white. Of sauours, the sweete with adstriction. Of Countreys the Sea coastes of Asia the lesser, Cyprus, Media, Persia, Campanie, Rhetia, Sweathland, Lorraine, Bolongne, Sene, Montorie, Tarrante, Parme, Panorme, Capne, Salerne, Verone, and the vi. Climate. Of particuler places, Feildes, Tillages, Vines very neere greene, Gardens, and other pleasant and odoriferous places.

Gemini gouerneth ouer the right parte of Occident, ouer the ayre, ouer the blood, and other end of the spring time, ouer the shoulders, armes, and handes. And signifieth men of middle stature, fayre faced, and bodyed, store of haire, little eyes, labouring men, subtile, ingenious, prudent teachers, fraudulent, Arethmetricians, Geometricians, Astrologians, Orators, Poets, Aduocates, Witches, Southsayers, Busie fellowes, Weauers. Of sicknesses, Phleames, Foroncles, and others comming of blood in the sayd parte. Of Colours, the mixtures. Of Sauors, the sweete. Of Countreyes, Hircanye, Armenie, Montiane, Syrenianq;, Marmariq;, Lowe Egipte, England, Sordigne, Brabant, Flaunders, Lombardie, Viterbie, Vercel, Norremberge, Louayne, Magonce, Brudges, London, Paris, Cordube. Of particular places, Fayres, Schooles, Shoppes, places of high mountaines, places of hunting of birdes, places garnished within with instruments of musique.

Cancer gouerneth the heart of the Septentrion, ouer the water, ouer the hollow humours, and Phlegmatiques,

ouer

ouer the breft, fides, and lunges, and ouer the dugges and ftomacke. And fignifieth amiable men, peaceable, modeft, white, full faced, the nofe indifferent long, lardge fhoulders, little bearded, flowthfull, vnconftant, and effeminate, Nauigators, Strangers, Confulls, Attcurnies, &c. Of difeafes, Litargy, Leproufie, darkeneffe of the fight, galling of the skinne, and euill fickneffes, of the face and bodie. Of Colours, the white and yellow. Of fauours, the falt, and his contrary frefhnes. Of Countries, Bythinie, Phrigia, Affrica, Carthage, Scotland, the kingdome of Grenade, the Countie of Burgony, Prufie, Holland, Zelande, Conftantinople, Thunis, Venis, Millayne, Genes, Luques, Pife, Treues, Madebourge, Berne: Of particular places: pondes, lakes, riuers, the fea, and portes of the fea.

Leo, gouerneth the left parte of Orient, ouer the fire, ouer the choller, ouer the heart, ftomacke, liuer and backe. And fignifieth fayre men, ftraight, the nofe broade and little, great eares, with a little ftrong looke, the face browne, the body reddifh, hairy, couragious and of great heart, Princes, Officers, Magiftrates, Gouernours Kings. Of difeafes, fhaking of the heart, fwoundings. Of Colours the yellow and redde as golde. Of fauors, the bitter, and the ftrong. Of Countries, Italie, Fraunce, Apulie, Sicillia, Chaldea, Bohemia, Rome, Rauenna, Prage, Vlme, Mantoue, Cremone, Syracufa: Of particular places, noble landes, Lordfhips, Caftels Townes, Pallaces, and Royall buildings.

Virgo gouerneth ouer the right part of the Meridies, ouer the earth, ouer the malancholly, ouer the gutts, belly and diaphragme: And fignifieth men of indifferent greatnes, the bodie ftraight, the face fayre, good voyce, fhining haire, little eyes, prudent, learned, ingenious, couetous of glorie and honour, Scriueners, Arithmeticians, Geometricians, Boate men. Of difeafes, the collique, (the difeafe which caufeth the patient to vomit his excremēts at his mouth called Iliaque) &c. Of Colours, the white

I   and

& purple: of fauours the aftringēt: of Countries,Greece, Achaia,Creet,Mefopotania,Affiria,Cicilia, Athēs,Rodes, Alexandria,Hierufalē,Corinth,Tarrante, Beneuent, Farrare,Pauia,Baffe, Paris , Lyons, Tholofe. Of particular places,faires: fhops: fchooles : and arrable grounds.

Libra gouerneth ouer the hart of the Occident,ouer the aire,ouer the blood,ouer the beginning of Autume,& ouer the reynes : and denoteth fimple mē,honorable, faire faced with whitnes ouer al the body,the eyes a little troubled or fpoyled,plaiers,dauncers,mufitiās,hunters,iudges. Of difeafes,fuppreffiō of the vrine,iffue of blood in the lower parts,ftones in the reynes,& darknes of the eyes. Of colours,the greene : of fauours, fweete : of Regions Bactriane, Cafpie, Thebes, Trogloditiq; , Ethiopia, Tufcia, Auftria, Sauoy, Danphina, Gaiete, Plaifance,Argenton, Vienna in Auftria,Franckford,Spire,Augufte,Arles,Lifbone.Of particular places,where fuites be iudged vppon, all high places and mountaynes bearing corne,grapes, or other fruites.

Scorpio gouerneth ouer the left part of the Septentrion : ouer the water : ouer the phlegmatiq; humours and aquofits,ouer the parts dedicated to generation. And fignifieth men very deformed : broad brefted : the head deformed: great fpeakers: bablers: mockers: lyers: gluttons: voluptuous: traytors: fpyes: poyfonnours. Of difeafes,darkneffe of the eyes: fcabbes: fcurffes: kanckers: leoproufneffe: falling off the hayre: and deformed difeafes in the face: and all the bodie impoyfoned by violence of medicines,&c. Of colours, the redde and tawnie. Of fauours,falt and frefh. Of Regions,Syria,Cappadocia: the lande of the Moores: Catalongne: Bauaires: Trapezonce: Saxonie: Padua : Vrbin: Brixie: Valence in Spaine: Vienna in Danphinna. Of particular places, vineyardes : and gardens euill trimmed, defert places: ftincking: infected: abounding in woormes: fnakes: and fcorpions,&c.

Sagitarius gouerneth ouer the right parte of the O-
rient,

rient : ouer the fire : ouer choller : ouer the end of Au-
tumme : ouer the thighes : and all superfluous partes :
as a sixth part of the finger &c. And representeth men
of right and high stature : the face yellowe or reddish,
the brest large : Cattes eyes : iust men and pittifull : & ce-
remonious : iudges : magistrates : prelats : beneficed men
marchants, hunters. Of diseases, darknes of the eyes, falles
from high places : hurts by horses : Agues & woundes.
Of colours : cleere : yellow. Of sauours : strong & sharp
with some sweetnes intermingled: of Countries, Tuscan,
Spayne : Arabia the happye : Portugale : Hungarie :
Slauonia : Volterre : Mutine : Bude : Caschonia : Nar-
bona : Auignon : Tolete. Of particular places , Gardens : Wayes : Mountaynes : or where menne keepe
horses.

Capricorne gouerneth ouer the heart of the meridies,
ouer the earth : melanchollie : the knees : ouer the beginning of the Winter. And signifieth little stature, a
little rounde head : the face browne : faire nose : fayre
eyes : chollerique and sadde : subtle : secrete : prudent :
paynefull : sheepheards : fishers : marryners : carpenters :
buyers of Rentes. Of diseases, scabbes : gaules : infirmyties of the skinne : hinderaunces of the hearing : of
the voyce : of the eyes : issues of blood in the lower parts.
Of colours blacke and earthly. Of sauours, the bitter
and astringent. Of Regions, Macedonia, Thracia, Indea,
Brandebourge : Anchone : Fauence : Tortonne : Aus-
burge, Conslans, Gand, Malnies. Of particular places,
Gardens, Fountaynes, Riuers, Fields tilled, Land plowed,
Prisoners, Caues, Obscure places, deepes; and full of
fewines and vapours.

Aquarius gouerneth ouer the left parte of the Occident, ouer the ayre, ouer the blood, ouer the legges, o-
uer the middle of Winter. And signifieth fayre men,
fayer & somwhat long faced, & the face somwhat red, the
brest or the elbowes marked, and men Curteous, Scotia-
ble, Couetous, Prudent, giuen to the actes of Saturnins.

Of diseases, quarterne feuers, the blacke iaunders, &c. Of Colours, the greene and darke yellow. Sauours, sweete. Of Countries, Arabia, Ethiopia, Sarmatia, Oxione, Tartaria, Denmarke, Piemount, Mountferrat, Pisaure. Of particular places, Lakes, Pondes, Close places, Caues, Sepulchers and infamous houses.

Pisces gouerneth ouer the right part of the Septentrion ouer the water, phlegme, aquisits, and ouer the feete, and ouer the end of winter. And signifieth men of whitish colour, delicate, faire foreheaded, fayre breasted, faire bearded, the eyes open and indifferent great, and indifferent sickly: Fishers, and Nauigators. Of diseases, gaules vppon the skinne, vlcers and deformed spottes vppon the skinne payne in the feete. Of Colours, the greene, white & mixtures. Of sauors salt and fresh. Of Regions, Lydia, Lycia, Cicilia, Pamphilia, Calabria, Normandie: Rattisbone: Roane: Compostella, Of particular places: port of the Sea: heades of Riuers, Pondes and watrish places.

Chap. III.
Of that which the Plannets signifie in the sayde Signes.

SAturne in his signes of Capricorne and Aquarius in Natiuities by day giueth knowledge and loue of noble men: and of credit and great riches principally in the Ascendant: with the part of Fortune: and maketh the man graue, prudent: proude and melianchollie: and first of all his bretheren, or most aduaunced. In Natiuities by night giueth great payne and trauayle and many diseases. Iupiter in the sayd signe, maketh the man of little courage, vnfortunate in the goodes of the Church, otherwise of small riches, or alwayes poore.

Mars maketh him bolde, a great enterpriser of matters, and not in vayne, and maketh him see the death of his bretheren.

The Sunne in the natiuities by day signifieth that hee shall be perfect and happie in all his enterprises. In natiuities

tiuities by night that he shall haue vnconstant fortune.

Venus maketh him an Adulterer and effeminate, and denoteth that his wiues shall not liue long.

Mercurie causeth him to haue impeachment in his tongue, and maketh the man euill spoken otherwise, and which haunteth the companie of men of knowledge and of Religion.

The Moone maketh the man too slowthfull, and one of euill estimation : and his mother also , and signifieth imbicillitie of the eyes and great coughes.

In the houses of Iupiter. ♃ ♓

Saturne in the houses of Iupiter, which bee Sagitarius & Pisces maketh the man fayer, rich, mighty and faithfull in natiuities by day: In natiuities by night, strife against men of authoritie, and neere the death of his Father.

Iupiter signifieth riches, honour, great creditte and offices.

Mars yeeldeth the men noble, gouernours in warres & friendes of Princes.

The Sunne maketh them beneficed men, prelats, officers and more aduaunced then any of their familie, they shalbe alwayes greatly couetous.

Venus giueth them goodes of the Church, or of the side of women; and maketh them discreet, honest, among the which they shall haue great strife against theyr parents, famylies and friendes.

Mercurie maketh them iust, men of good estimation, which by their proper vertue shall come to the knowledge & loue of great Lordes and Kings.

The Moone yeeldeth them chiefe and most honored among their friendes : maketh them also couetous, found and of long life.

In the house of Mars. ♈ ♏

Saturne giueth great anger and cruell malice.

Iupiter maketh the man happie, and a friende of great

lords

Lordes, and a Conductor of warres, principall in the signe of Aries.

Mars within his houses signifieth Captaines, Gouernours in warres, and great Lordes.

The Sunne, hote diseases, in the signe of Scorpi : in the signe of Aries great aduauncement.

Venus denoteth luxurie and all voluptuous villanie, but against nature, and euill dealing to women. Alwayes in the signe of Aries she maketh him hate women, principally if the moone be in the same signe, and if the sunne be in a masculine signe.

Mercurie, maketh the man a lyer, an euill person, a deceiuer, a babler and a demaunder of vniust thinges : otherwise eloquent, subtle in his affayres, diligent, suspicious, a nigromancer, a little false or a theefe.

The moone denoteth euill companions, in perill of being drowned : and short end by the sea.

In the houses of the Sunne. ♌

Saturne in the signe of Leo : being a house of the Sunne : sygnifieth good Fortune and long life to the father.

Iupiter maketh the man wise : of good spirite : of good nature : amiable : which by vertue shall come to the knoweledge and loue of great Kinges and princes.

Mars denoteth violent death, great sicknesses, losse of goodes, infirmyties of the eyes, and of the Stomacke.

The Sunne in his sayde house signifieth great and incredible aduauncement, in Angles or Houses succedant, when the Natiuitie is by daye : VVhen it is by night sygnifieth Sadnesse, Enuies, and a short ende of the Father.

Venus, great loue, great couetousnes, and impudent life, when Iupiter dooth not regard her.

Mercurie: good writers, men of knowledge, good memorie, and of great councell.

The

The moone, honourable companions, and viuacitie of the ſpirite.

In the houſes of Venus. ♉ ♎

Saturne denoteth impudent life, loue of maydes & women of ſmall diſcretion, diſeaſes by reaſon of leacherie.

Iupiter honourable companions, loue of great lordes, profit by the ſide of women, or Eccleſiaſticall goodes, or comming by the men of the Church.

Mars, furious men, raueſhers of women, ſhameleſſe in their leacherie, vnto the conſtraynings of their parents & friendes.

In the ſigne of Taurus, maketh the man, falſe and trayterous.

In the ſigne of Libra denoteth ſome hurt by irō or fire.

The Sunne maketh him contēplatiue, iuſt, interperter of dreames, curious in the ſecreets of nature, and a louer of pilgrimages.

Venus ſignifieth ioyfulnes, great proſperity, happy in effecting his enteprifes, but he ſhal loue womē reprehended Mercurie giueth many good & profitable friendes : and yeeldeth the man pleaſant, ioyfull, and a muſitian.

The moone giueth profit by women.

In the houſes of Mercurie. ♊ ♍

Saturne, maketh the man verye skilfull, wiſe, and of great iudgement : which hath enuious menne purſuing him, an impediment in his ſpeach, his anger violent.

Iupiter maketh him alſo skilfull, or a marchant, a man of good fayth, and more rich then his parents.

Mars, ſlowthfull, prudent, ſubtile, men of warre.

Sagitarius buſie fellowes, counterfeytors of letters and forgers.

The ſunne giueth aboundance of knowledge aſwell in matters of iudgements as in mathematickes.

Venus companies & loue of men of the Church, otherwiſe ſhe doth yeelde them very leacherous.

Mercurie in his proper houses signifieth men of all knowledge, philosophers, mathematicians: Orators, Aduocates, Poets, Rimers Southsayers, & skilfull in knauery.

The Moone good life and long, great vnderstanding in the affayers which he taketh in hande, good fortune in merchandizes and in loue of young maydens.

In the house of the Moone.

Saturne greate sicknesse losse of goodes: hurt in the eyes, voyages from the which hee shall neuer returne, or very late with great payne.

Iupiter: loue of honourable men good renowne and good fortune.

Mars: swiftnesse of spirit, rash, bold enterprisers, blindnes of the eyes, losse of goodes by his mother.

The Sunne, good renowne, and if he be ioyned to the tayle of the Dragon, or to Saturne or Mars, blindnesse of eyes, perill of drowning, frequenting voiages.

Venus signifieth, inconstancy, & shamlesse lecherie.

Mercurie good will, chastitie, fidelitie, and happie fortune in deedes of marchandise.

The Moone, holly, and profitable in voiagaes, Traffiques and marchandize when she is fortunate: or when she is vnfortunate, continuall sicknesses, hurts in the eyes, perill of death by land and water

Chap. IIII.
Of the aspects of the Plannets betweene them.

THE Coniunctiõ of Saturne & Iupiter giueth faire possessions, farmes rents, houses, & charges of the affaires of the king, profitable if Mars do not behold them.

The coniunction of Saturne & Mars, signifieth that the child shalbe trusted: but he shal not accomplish his enterprises without great difficulty, & shall die sooner then his father & mother, & yet his brethren shall die before him.

The

The coniunction of Saturne and of the Sunne, losse of patrimony, great trauaile to gette goods, and most in the natiuities by night.

The coniunction of Saturne and Venus, denote that the man shal haue no male chyldren, that he shal espouse some old woman, or some widdowe, or some of euil condition, or a bastard: or other staine of hys honour, or by the which his parents haue had some discredite.

The coniunction of Saturne and Mercury, doth yeelde him a poore vagabonde, needy, of no mistery, the which hath an impediment in hys speech.

The coniunction of Saturne and Luna, weakenes of bodie, losse by the side of his Parents.

The coniunction of Iupiter & Mars, signifieth, riches, rule and gouernment of warres, and of good renowne.

The coniunction of Iupiter and the Sunne, pouerty & neede if it be not Orientall, for then it promiseth good fortune to the father, to hym, and to his children.

The coniunction of Iupiter and Venus, good institution, amity of honourable men, and profit of them, and of the wife and chyldren.

The coniunction of Iupiter and Mercury, signifieth Lawyers, Secretaries and Chauncellers.

The coniunction of Iupiter & the Moone, great riches.

The coniunction of Mars and the Sunne, losse of patrimony, damage of goods, and short lyfe to the father, and great perrill of the child to be burnt.

The coniunction of Mars and Venus, sutes, strifes, debates by reason of women, adulterers with women of infamous condition.

The coniunction of Mars & Mercury, lyers, deceiuers, eloquent, dilligent, and bablers.

The coniunction of Mars and the Moone, shorte lyfe, woundes, blowes, danger of violent death by yron or by fier, or by falles and ruines.

The coniunction of Sol & Venus, praise, good renown, fauour of the common people, especially of women.

K   The

The coniunction of Sol & Mercurie, wisdom, science, great aduauncement, and estimation to be very skilfull.

The coniunction of the Sunne & of the Moone, short lyfe, gouernment, and honourable company.

The coniunction of Venus and Mercury, maketh the man pleasant, ioyfull, a player, a dauncer, musitian, well furnished, and bringeth hym damage by the side of women. If they be conioyned vnder the beames of the Sun, they make great hinderance in the parts of generation.

The coniunction of Venus & the Moone, maketh the man fayre, pleasant, proude, an adulterer: and of whom his wife is an adultresse, if Mars do cast his beames without aspect of Iupiter.

The coniunction of Mercury & Luna, denoteth good renowne, science, & vnconstancy of maners & of fortune.

The tryne aspect of Saturne and Iupiter, signifieth inheritaunces, possessions, faire houses, riches, meetings with treasures, great gaynes: whē they be infortuate places of the figure.

The tryne of Saturne and Mars, great aduauncement, dignities, great credite, rule and gouernment of townes & Countries, and death of brethren.

The tryne of Saturne and the Sunne, rule, offices, dignities, great renowne, in natiuities by day: in the night it maketh the dispersing of patrimony goods, & afterwards by his deedes and vertue shall recouer and obtaine more greater.

The tryne of Saturne & Venus, maketh the man trustie, milde, honest, shame-faced, of good conuersation, of good renowne, the which by men of base condition shall be pursued with enuie, and shall marry late.

The tryne of Saturne and Mercurie, maketh the man prudent, subtile in all his affayres, a man of good & great knowledge, ingenious, industrious, an Arithmetrician, Geomitrician, Astrologian, and a Geographer, President in matters of accounts and calculations: Chauncellors, Secretaries and Registers.

The

The tryne of Saturne & of the Moone, fauour of great Lords and Kings, glory, honour and gouernment.

The tryne of Iupiter and Mars, signifieth audacity, honour, victory, fauour of Kings, gouernment of townes & great credite.

The tryne of Iupiter and Sol being greatly fauourable, to glory, honour, gouernment, credite, and giueth great riches, fayre possesions, and fayre chyldren.

The tryne of Iupiter & Venus, denoteth beauty, grace, faithfulnes, honesty, and profit of wiues and friends, dignities and inheritaunces by theyr meanes.

The tryne of Iupiter and Mercurie , maketh the man ingenious, subtile, forward, of good iudgement & aduise, happy in his enterprises, a Iudge, Officer, great Lord, Secretary, well vnderstanding the secretes of nature and Astrologie.

The tryne of Iupiter with the Moone, signifieth noblenesse, honour, glory, good renowne, loue of vertue, fidelity, principality and gouernment.

The tryne of Mars with the Sunne, great aduancement, great credite, dignities, gouernments administrations of Common-wealthes, and Conductors of warres.

The tryne of Mars with Venus, gayne, riches, goods of women, proude, arrogant, braue and lecherous.

The tryne of Mars and Mercurie, prudent, crafty, subtile of spyrite , and maketh the man to studie secretly: a good Aduocate, President in matters of account, & rich.

The tryne of Mars with Luna, maketh him happy in all his affaires: President in matters of account, an honorable officer, & a great Lord, with great renowne.

The trine of the Sunne with Venus, signifieth the same that the tryne of Mars and Venus signifieth, with great honour of the said significations.

The tryne of the Sun with Mercury and Luna, likewise as of Mars, with great honour and profit.

The tryne of Venus with Mercurie, braue , pleasant, graue, beauty, and happy enterprises with profit.

The tryne of Venus & the Moone, beauty, grace, brauerie, pride, and adultery.

The tryne of Mercury with the Moone, maketh the
man greatly esteemed in hys profession : be it in musicke,
paynting, or other pleasant industry : or in al knowledge,
or in merchandise or office.

The Sextiles aspects, make the same effects which the
trynes make ; except that the Sextiles bee not of so perfect vertue.

The Quadrate aspect of Saturne and Iupiter, signifieth
losse of patrimoniall goods, great aduersities, hinderaunces in all enterprises : vaine cogitations, principally when
Saturne is eleuated ouer Iupiter, without receiuing hym.

The quadrate of Saturne and Mars, signifieth asmuch,
and further maketh knowne the death of brethren.

The quadrate of Saturne and the Sunne out of the sayd
significations, bringeth great damage to the honour, and
spoyleth the body with cold diseases and contractions of
the sinowes; and maketh the father die before the mother, and yeeldeth the chyld not agreeable to his father.

The quadrate of Saturne with Venus, denoteth losse
of goods, pouertie, myserable fortune to women, vnciui-
lity, when Saturne holdeth the right part of the aspect.
For when Venus holdeth it, the chyld shall be shame faced and of good manners, and hys wiues shall loue hym
effectually, although they dissemble theyr loue and wyll
gouerne in the house.

The quadrate of Saturne & Mercury, maketh the man
laborous, a seruaunt, of poore councell, deafe or of ill hearing, stutting or euill spoken, pursued of enuie.

The quadrate of Saturne and of the Moone, maketh
the man slothfull, sickly, euill graced, full of care, without
friendes, a disperser of the goods of hys mother and of his
wiues.

The quadrate of Iupiter and Mars, if Iupiter be migh-
tiest, it signifieth that the chyld shall be esteemed, praised
and honoured of Princes & Kings, and that he shall haue
perseue-

perfeueraunce in all hys enterprifes with profit; alwayes he fhal lofe and dyfperfe his inheritances and poffefsions, and fhall fee the death or deftruction of his children. If *Mars* be moft eleuate, he fignifieth futes,debates and lof-fes, by meanes of great Lords, and a troublefome lyfe.

The quadrate of Iupiter with the Sunne,if Iupiter bee the Superior, honour,profit,and good fortune to the Fa-ther. If the Sunne be Superior, the child fhal difperfe his goods,and fhall not be beloued of hys neighbours; and fhall goe out of his Country.

The quadrate of Iupiter and Venus, profit by women, faithfulnes,honefty,ciuility,when Iupiter is moft higheft. When he is inferiour, luft,deceite by women, inconftan-cie, ioy incontinently turned into fadnes, when Venus is not receiued by Iupiter.

The quadrate of Iupiter and *Mercury*, fignifieth the man skilfull, a Mathematician,a Sorcerer, Sooth-fayer, a-bounding in feruaunts, very faythfull and very rich,prin-cipally when Mercurie is receyued by Iupiter.

The quadrate of Iupiter and the *Moone*, of good re-nowne, great honours, in knowledge and loue of great Lords, with a little vnconftant of Fortune and of maners.

The quadrate of *Mars* with the Sunne, fignifieth ma-ny euils,loffe of goods, darknes of the eyes, and in great daunger of violent death,or publique.

The quadrate of *Mars* with Venus, great troubles & tribulations by reafon of women of bafe condition,or im-pudent,& fomewaies defamed,when *Mars* is in a moue-ble figne.

The quadrate of *Mars* with *Mercurie*, weakenes of all the body, pryfons,purfutes, accufations, falfe nature of the chyld, wyth malice and iniquitie.

The quadrate of *Mars* and the *Moone*, fignifieth the mother to be weake, and of a very fhort lyfe,and the child an euill boy, prodigall, vnconftant,poore, and which fhal die myferably : and of the which, the wiues fhalbe proud, arrogant,and terrible.

The

The quadrate of the Sunne and Venus, signifieth that which the quadrate of Iupiter and Venus signifieth.

The quadrate of Sol & Mercury, signifieth that which the quadrate of Iupiter and Mercury signifieth.

The quadrate of the Sunne with the Moone, augmenteth the dignities and the honors,& giueth enuiousnes.

The quadrate of Venus and Mercury,maketh the man diligent & industrious in his office,& well renowned,but he shal receiue some infamy by reason of women.

The quadrate of Venus and Luna maketh him verie rich,and happy in his profession, eloquent,gracious,very happy in wiues & chyldren : but hee shal haue some losse of good and honour by reason of women.

The quadrate of Mercury with Luna,maketh him skilfull, ingenious , vnconstant of manners and of fortunes, which in a common sedition shall be taken, or shal be accused by many of his conspirators.

The Opposition of Saturne & Iupiter, signifieth great troubles,a thousande mischiefes and tribulations, depriued of chyldren. If Saturne be in the ascendant,and Iupiter in the seauenth house, the beginning of hys life shall bee with paynes, trybulations and torments,and the ende with repose, profite and honour.

The opposition of Saturne and Mars without aspect of Iupiter and Venus,denote great troubles, common seditions and conspyrations against the sayd man : many dyseases intollerable, ruines, falles, perrils by water, violent death,or pestilence, and a miserable father.

The opposition of Saturne and Sol without aspect of Iupiter,maketh the man sickly,sad, full of thoughts, full of tribulations, with great losse of goods, and daunger of violent death.

The opposition of Saturne and Venus , maketh hym euill disposed, depriued of beauty and of vertue, lecherous, infamous by reason of women.

The opposition of Saturne and Mercury, an imperfect speech,seperation of brethren,knowledge and science.

The

The oppofition of Saturne and Luna, difpertion of hys mothers goods, gryefes happening to the mother, troubles and tribulations, with great danger of violent death, according to the nature of the figne wherein Luna is.

The oppofition of Iupiter and Mars, rafhnes, difpertion of goods, enemy to them which haue beene friendes, vnconftant fortune.

The oppofition of Iupiter & Sol, maketh him difperfe his fathers goods, & fell his offices and his honor.

The oppofition of Iupiter and Venus, fignifieth vnconftant friendes, vngratitude of them where hee hath doone good: otherwife fufficient fortune.

The oppofition of Iupiter and Mercurie, common feditions, enuies, confpirations, ftrifes, futes, enmitie of brethren, of the which he fhall fee the death.

The oppofition of Iupiter with Luna, fufficient fortune after long trauaile.

The oppofition of Mars and of the Sunne, fpoyle of the eyes, maketh him to be killed, or fal from on high, maketh him difperfe his patrimony, & his father die quickly.

The oppofition of Mars and Venus, yeeldeth the man voluptuous, an a little vicious, weak, vnconftant, and maketh his wife and children to die in fignes tropiques, maketh him marry wiues of bafe condition, or otherwife defamed.

The oppofition of Mars and Mercury, without afpect of Iupiter, maketh the man a falfefyer, of euill confcience, accompanied with euil chyldren, accufed of many crimes, for the which hee fhall be a fugitiue or banifhed: principally if Mercury be in the houfes of Saturne.

The oppofition of Mars and the Moone, fignifieth fpoyle of the eyes and the body, by blowes and hurts and other ficknefses, and gyueth great aduerfities, maketh him hate marriage, and caufeth violent death, and often Canon: principally when the Moone increafeth in the angles, wyth fufficient afpect of fortunes.

The oppofition of the Sun, of Venus and of Mercurie, fignifie signifie that which we haue sayd of Iupiter.

The opposition of the Sunne and of the Moone, changeth the fortunes of goods and honour, pouertie after riches, dishonour after honour, weakenes of bodie after health; mutation of good to euill,and great vnconstancie of manners.

The opposition of Venus and Mercury, enuies, quarrels, enmities by reason of women; otherwise graue eloquence, beauty and brauery.

The opposition of Venus with the Moone, vnfortunate marriage, iniuries by women,depryuation of chyldren.

The opposition of Mercury and of the Moone, conspyrations against hym, enuies, treasons, feare and lecherous.

Likewise you must regarde the parte of Fortune, the part of the Spyrite, and of theyr aspects with the sayde Planets; you must iudge as of the aspects of the Planets with the Sunne and the Moone. For if the parte of fortune be part of the Moone, and part of the Spirit & part of the Sunne, which would consider the aspects towards the other parts and houses of heauen, he may iudge as of the Planets of the which the proiections of the sayd parts shall be made. &c.

C H A P. V.

Of the significations of the twelue houses.

THE first house signifieth the life,nourishment,and disposition of the body of the spirit, and complexion, and representeth the head,face, brayne, eares, and nose, and is called, Horyscope angle, adorning and ascending.

The second house signifieth goods, traffique, ryches, gayne,companies to gette profite & gayne men that help to gayne. It signifyeth also gold and siluer, and al moueable goods,and is called, The house succedant to the ascendant, and beneath the earth; & raigneth ouer the neck.

The

The thyrd houſe denoteth the brethren, ſiſters, Coſins and allies, and little voyages, and the lyuer, and diuinations of dreames, and is called, The houſe cadant of the aſcendant, otherwiſe goodnes : and hath gouernment ouer the ſhoulders, legges and armes.

The fourth houſe ſignifieth the Fathers and Parents poſſeſsions, inheritaunces, houſes, fieldes, Orchards, vineyardes labouring, woode, and other goods & moueables, treaſures and goods hydden, and mynerall matters, pryſons and obſcure places, and in the end all things ; & that which commeth after death, as the graue and good reporte. &c. and is called, The angle of the earth, and the depth thereof : and raigneth ouer the breſt and lunges.

The fift houſe ſignifieth infancie and Daughters, Nepheues, gyfts, preſents, pleaſures, voluptuouſnes, ornanaments, brauerie, dauncing, playes, banquetting, meſſages, gold and ſiluer, and the riches of the Father, the profite of inheritaunces, poſſeſſions, tyllage, and is called, The houſe ſuccedant to the fourth, and otherwiſe good fortune : and raigneth ouer the hart and ſtomack.

The ſixt houſe denoteth ſeruaunts, ſicknes, wild beaſts, ryding, hunting of and by dogges : ſheepe and muttons, Goates and Pulleine, and hath ſome ſignification ouer pryſons, vniuſtice, and falſe accuſations, and is called, The houſe cadant of the fourth, and otherwiſe euil fortune, and hath gouernment ouer the belly and bowels.

The ſeauenth houſe, denoteth marriage, wiues, ſutes, quarrels, ſtryfe, debate, knowne enmity, and men appertayning to gayne and profite, and ſignifieth agedneſſe, and ſtrange places, & is called, The angle of the occident, and raigneth ouer the reynes.

The eyght houſe ſignifieth ſadnes, enuie, long torments, the quality of death : dowery with wiues, inheritance and other benefit, prouided by Parents, and thoſe that belong to gayne, riches of the which one hath not greatly thought, and is called, The houſe ſuccedant, to the angle occidentall, and otherwiſe is entred on high, and

L   gouer-

gouerneth the parts of generation.

The nynth, long viages : long pilgrimages and nauigations : fayth : religion : sacrifices : cerimonies : science : wisedome : diuination of dreames : prodigious interpretations : new sects : paradoxes : signes of heauen : diuine punishment : and is called, The house Cadant of the angle occidentall, and otherwise the house of God, and gouerneth the buttocks.

The tenth, signifieth honour : dignities : offices : Magistrates : administrations : gouernment : Rulers : Conductors : good renowne : estimation : profession : action : and the mother : and is called, The middle and heart of heauen : the Merydian poynt and angle Merydian. It gardeth and gouerneth the knees.

The eleuenth house, signifieth friendes : companions : hope : confidence : fauour : helpe : succour : prayse : estimation and renowne : counsell of friends : and is called, The house succedant to the angle Meridional, and otherwise called the good angle : and gouerneth the legges.

The twelfe house signifieth hidden enemies : prysons : captiuitie : bondage : sadnes : torment : complaynt : lamentation : teares and hate; treasons : villanies : horses and great beastes of lyke and iust proportion : and is called, The house cadant of the angle Meridional, & otherwise an euill spyrite : and gouerneth the feete.

CHAP. VI.
Of the Lords of the Triplicities of the said
Houses.

THE first Lorde of the tryplicitie of the first angle, denoteth the nature and life of the chylde, and hys cogitations and will : that which he loueth and hateth, and that which is to come, health or sicknesse : good or euill entertainment, perrill of his life in the first age. The second, Lord of the tryplicitie of the saide angle, signifieth force and strength of the body, & the midst of the lyfe.

The

The thyrd, the end of the lyfe.

The firſt Lord of the tryplicitie of the ſeconde houſe, betokeneth riches, the ſecond the manner of the ſame riches, the third the intent and confidence in getting.

The firſt Lord of the tryplicitie of the thyrd houſe, denoteth the moſt auncient and fyrſt brethren, the ſeconde the middle, the third the leaſt.

The firſt Lord of the fourth, denoteth the Parents, the ſecond lands poſſeſsions and houſes, the thyrd impriſonment and end of things.

The firſt Lord of the fyft, denoteth chyldren, the ſecond loue, pleaſure, grace and brauery, the third, meſſages and embaſſages.

The firſt Lorde of the ſixt houſe, denoteth ſickneſſe, trouble, the ſecond, ſeruaunts, the thyrd, Cattell, pryſon, and the profite of the ſignifications of the ſaid houſe.

The fyrſt of the ſeauenth houſe, women, the ſeconde ſtrife and ſute, the thyrd diuiſion.

The fyrſt Lord of the eyght houſe, death, the ſeconde, antiquity, the thyrd, inheritaunce.

The fyrſt Lord of the ninth houſe, denoteth pilgrimages, long viages, nauigations: the ſecond, fayth, religion, and deuotion: the thyrd, ſcience, deuination, dreames, prophecies, ſortes of croſſe and prodigall ſects.

The fyrſt of the tenth, denoteth profeſſion, honor, dignitie and aduauncements: the ſecond, audacitie, and the meanes to work in his profeſſion: & the third, preſeruation in ſuch fortune.

The fyrſt of the eleuenth houſe, denoteth conſtancie, hope, the ſecond, friendes: the thyrde, the profite of the eleuenth houſe.

The fyrſt of the twelfe houſe, denoteth enemies: the ſecond, payne and trauaile: the thyrd, beaſtes of like proportion: and other that be appoynted to charge and labour.

IN the first house, Saturne out of his principall dignities, signifieth that the chyld shall haue short life, vnfortunate, deformed, euill-fauoured : and shall dye because of other lands and possessions : neuerthelesse, he
shall be first of his bretheren.

Iupiter in the sayd house signifieth long life, good fortune, beauty, honesty, loue of vertue, feare of God, honour, and fauour, and makes hym the first of hys Bretheren.

Mars in the sayde place, signifieth hurt alwaies in the
heade or face, and maketh hym dispende a parte of hys
goods, and maketh him intermeddle in many dyscordes
and contentions : if he be in his house or exaltation, it maketh him a mighty and valiant man, hardy, fortunate in
armes. out of his principall dignities, it dooth yeelde hym
euill, mischieuous, furious, seditious, mutinous and quar-
relsome : principally when the fortunes do not intermingle theyr beames.

The Sunne gyueth honour and prayse, and estimation,
credite and great aduauncement : fauour of great Lords,
riches by the meanes of Princes, and maketh the chylde
first borne, or most aduaunced of all his bretheren.

Venus gyueth hym grace, beauty, brauery, ciuility, loue
of women, healthfull and prosperous : and yeeldeth the
man lecherous, ioyous, louing musick, dauncing, & something vnconstant.

Mercurie, maketh hym ingenious, skilfull, dilligent,
Apprentice, of good iudgement, of good memory, a good
Reader, a good Wryter, a great Mathematician ; and apt
to all knowledge.

The Moone yeeldeth hym vnconstant, vagabond, which
taketh diuers affayres, and given to many viages, a man
healthfull, fortunate, fayre, & something spotted in the
face,

face, and fhall be numbred among great Lords.

The head of the Dragon lunarie, honour, dignity and fauour of great Lords & Prelates. The tayle of the Dragon, loffe of goods and honour, deformity, obfcurenes of eyes, and great danger of the loffe of lyfe.

In the fecond houfe Saturne out of his principall dignities, deftroyeth the man, and maketh him fpende and fcatter his goods, and yeeldeth him poore and vnprouided of fuccour. And in his houfe or exaltation, maketh him rich, proude, and with all his goods miferable.

Iupiter gyueth great riches by honeft meanes.

Mars maketh hym fpend his goods, & in the end doth yeeld him poore many waies.

Sol maketh hym honourable, a great man, liberal, braue, which in his magnificence fhall fpend his goods.

Venus giueth ayde and fuccour, and greatly enricheth by women and men of the Church.

Mercurie, profit in merchandize, and in Scripture, and very induftrious in the Mathematiques, and a thoufande meanes to become rich.

Luna, riches, aduauncement by embaffages, meffages, and imployments when fhe is fortunate; vnfortunate, fignifyeth paines and trauailes for the goods of the worlde, without going forward, and hynderaunce in whatfoeuer he doth.

The head of the Dragon, riches, great gaines, profit, inheritaunce, or goods of the Church.

The tayle of the Dragon, deftruction, prodigalitie, follie, difpence in playing, and falling from on high, without expectation.

In the third houfe, Saturne deftroyeth bretheren, and maketh them fee theyr death, and intermedleth ftryfes & futes among bretheren. Yeeldeth a man vnfortunate in fmall viages, an hypocrite, fuperfticious, rafh, fearefull aftonied at prodigious dreames.

Iupiter fignifieth peace & concord amongft bretheren, not without profite, maketh a man prudent, happy in

viages

viages neere hand, and that his dreames shall be true.

Mars signifieth great iniuries, strifes, and sutes among bretheren, and causeth the bretheren to die quickly: and yeeldeth the man a terrible blasphemer, forsworne, a deceiuer, not fearing GOD, which shall be vnfortunate in all his waies, and after in danger of Theeues and Robbers, and shall be tormented in many terrible and vaine dreames.

Sol, honour, dignities, offices, out of his Country, long pilgrimages, honourable bretheren, and true dreames.

Venus, loue among bretheren, happy viages, feare of God, and true dreames.

Mercurie, profite in traffique and viages, in fayre markets, and giueth good fortune at all times and places, concerning the good of the Church.

In the signe of Gemini or Libra, it maketh the man a good Musitian, and a sounder of musicall Instruments, principally in coniunction or good aspect of Venus.

The Moone maketh hym giuen to goe heere and there on pylgrimages, so that hee resteth not long in a place: neuerthelesse, in his deedes hee shall be honoured and prayfed, and meete with good fortune, and friendes, and great Lords, that shall employ him in embassages, in messages and other voyages: and hee shall be loued and prayfed of his bretheren.

The head of the Dragon signifieth, that his bretheren shall be of greater estate and authority then hee: neuerthelesse, it denoteth some Ecclesiasticall goods.

The tayle of the Dragon destroyeth the bretheren, & maketh them die quickly.

In the fourth house, Saturne out of his principall dignities, maketh him scatter his patrimony, and yeeldeth the man poore and vnfortunate in vnmooueable goods, as in houses, lands and possessions, plowing and sowing: and signifieth that the mother shalbe of an infamous condition, and shall not lyue long.

If hee be within his house or exaltation, hee gyueth inheriheritaunce, houfes, lands, poffefsions, and fignifieth the mother honorable, & of long life.

Iupiter, yeeldeth him happy in vnmooueable goods, & gyueth him great ftore of inheritaunce, & fometime caufeth him meete with treafure and goods, of the which he neuer greatly thought. And fignifieth the Father of long life and happy : and fignifieth hys chylde fhall be efteemed after hys death : and hee fhall be honourably layd in his graue.

Mars, loffe of goods by fier and wind, and houfes, lands and poffefsions, deftruction of trees, difpending of hys goods, euill end by wounds : effufion of bloode, euill renowne after death, and fhort life of the Father.

The Sunne denoteth faire poffefsions, lordfhips, gouernment, inheritaunce and fayre houfes, prayfe, honor and good fortune in hys olde yeeres, and good renowne after death, an honorable fepulchre, and maketh him gyuen to diuination, and to preuent things to come.

Venus denoteth the fame that Iupiter doth.

Mercury fortunate, yeeldeth the man induftrious, prouiding and forefeeing things to come : a buyer of rentes, houfes, and poffeffions, a planter of trees, and curious in Husbandry affayres : inclined to gather golde and filuer.

If it be vnfortunate, it yeeldeth hym quarrelfome, ftryuing, and hated of his neighbors, alwaies angry and ful of difpites, and little efteemed.

Luna fignifieth that which is faid of Mercurie, except that fhee is gyuen to Mylles, Pondes and watry places, and yeeldeth the man in the beginning vnfortunate, and in the ende happie, principallie when the natiuitie is by day.

And when the heade of the Dragon is in ayrie and fyerie Signes, it fignifyeth that which Iupiter dooth, and in earthly and watrie, that which the tayle of the Dragon dooth.

The tayle of the Dragon maketh the Father die quicklie, and fcatter his goods vnmoueable.

In

In the fift houfe, Saturne fignifyeth fadneffe, neceffitie, rudenes, vnciuill, euill-faced, euill entertainement, depriuation of death of chyldren vnnaturally, going in euil and filthy clothing.

Iupiter, gyueth grace, honefty, prudence, ciuility, brauerie, riches, profite in meffages and embaffages, aboundance of fayre chyldren, well nurtured, & well inftructed and beloued, good fortune by Churchmen, gyfts, and a dealer for gold, iewels, precious ftones, fweet and precious fauours.

Mars deftroyeth and maketh the chyldren die, or wholie depriueth them of chyldren: maketh a man happie in all fignifications of the fift houfe, when hee is out of hys principall dignities; Within his houfe or exaltation, he yeeldeth hym very lecherous and impudent, timerous, a fcoffer, abounding in baftards and euill chyldren.

The Sunne, denoteth fayre chyldren, honorable companies, good renowne, meffages, gyftes of great Lordes, and a dealer with Iewels and precious ftones, and fweete perfumes and fauours.

Venus maketh a man pleafant, delectable, ioyful, dauncing, vaunting, playing and laughing, Gentleman-like, a Mufitian, happy in children, lecherous and iealous.

Mercury maketh hym a merry iefter, a mocker, braue, to write well, a good Painter, induftrious with his handes, ingenious, a Mufitian, voluptuous, not caring greatly for his affayres or tribulations, indifferent happy in chyldren, and giuen to embaffages and meffages, and to goe on viages.

Luna maketh him an Atturney and of Councel, a Bencher, a Legate, an Embaffador by election of the people, and had in great account with the people, abounding in banquetting, and happy in chyldren.

The head of the Dragon fignifieth as Iupiter doth.

The tayle fignifieth what Mars and Saturne fignifie for chyldren.

In the fixt houfe, Saturne fignifieth payne of the belly and

and teeth,much ficknes, an ill feruaunt, vnlucky to fheep and like beaftes.

Iupiter,good feruaunts,health of the body,good Fortune in bringing vp beaftes.

Mars within his houfe or exaltation,good feruitours in warres, profeffion of phificke . Out of the fame places, hote ficknefles, peftilence, euill impediments, and euill feruaunts to be rebells, and theeues.

Sol, fickneffe of the heart, imbecillytie of the bodye, hurtes by his feruants.

Venus,imbicillytie of the Reynes and partes of generation, otherwife foundnes of body, good and faythfull feruaunts,good fortune in nourifhing beaftes, & commonlye impudent loue of maydes, and in natiuities of women maketh him loue feruaunts, and fignifieth perill of death in childe bearing.

Mercurie fignifieth him to be a deceiuer of women, & to be deceyued by them and his feruauutes, and yeeldeth him a deceyuer,a diffembler,a detefter,of euill memorye. If hee be with Saturne or Mars, hee threatneth death by pryfon , a confpiracie of feruants or in pryfon.

Luna denoteth weaknes in the eyes and brayne, great and feruent,ficknes,ftrife againft parents,enmytie of women,a company of men il condicioned,when fhe is infortunate. When fhe is fortunate, giueth health and profit in nourifhing young beaftes and good feruants.

The head of the Dragon preferueth from ficknes, giueth good feruants, and good lucke in keeping beaftes.

The tayle vnfaythfull feruauntes, loffe of cattell.

The feauenth, Saturne out of his principall dignities fignifieth marriage of an euill wife, blotted with fome infamie,proper to himfelfe or parents,ruine of enemyes, & perill of euill death. In watrie fignes it denoteth Emrods, Phiftyloes, Conftitution of the finewes, and difeafes of the backe,.

In his houfe or exaltation, hee fignifieth the woman to be rich,and enemies mightie.

M

Iupiter,

Iupiter, happy marriage, the woman honeſt, ſhamfaſte, vertuous, fayre, rich, victorie againſt enemies, & fortunate in age.

Mars in his houſe or exaltation, or out of his dignities alwayes ſignifieth myghty and terrible Aduerſaries, bruite of women, or husbandes in Natiuities of women, impudencye of the man, timerous, leacherous, in danger to be killed, to haue blowes on the feete & handes.

Sol, mighty enemie, rich, wiſe, well brought vp, and honourable age.

Mercurie, leachearous, ſtrife & debate betweene man and wife, euill by reaſon of impudent deſire, crafty knowledge in numbring, loue of vertue. If he be with Saturne or Mars hee ſhall kill his wife, and ſhall bee killed or put in pryſon, and put in exile, or condemned to dye by ſentence of a Iudge.

Luna, profit of wines, thouſand ſtrifes and ſuites, deſire of change of Countryes. If ſhee be fortunate, ſhe ſignifieth all well in all ſignifications of the ſayd houſe, and vnfortunate the contrary.

The head of the Dragon ſignifieth as Iupiter.

The tayle maketh the woman dye quickly & deſtroyeth the enemies.

In the eyght, Saturne out of his principall dignities, ſygnifieth ſtraunge Death, Sorrowes, Complaints, Lamentations, long Torments, Sadneſſe, Anguiſh & Pouertie in his houſe or exaltation, inheritaunce & goodes vnlooked for, death by flyxe or plague, or of ſome colde or long ſicknes.

Iupiter, long life to 72. yeares, inheritaunce, goodes by women, happy death.

Mars, out of his principall dignitie, ſignifieth haſtye death, peſtilence, impediment, ſlaughter, and other ſorts of violent death.

If he be with the head of the Dragō, he ſhalbe hanged, if in his houſe or exaltation he giueth goods not without great ſtriefes and ſuites.

Sol,

Sol, cauſeth death preſently after honor, ſhort life to the father, inheritaunce to the childe, loſſe of goodes by vyolence of great men, except when he is oppreſſed with çuill fortune, for then in an ayrie ſigne it ſignifieth ſtrangling by force, burned in fire, & kild, & buried in the earth, death by a fall, ruyne, drowning in water. Except in Scorpio, where it often cauſeth death by poyſon, mad doggs, or of venimous beaſtes.

Venus, good death, inheritaunce, riches, long life, ſhorte life of mother and Nurſe, and his wife more ancient then himſelfe.

Mercurie, enmytie of neighbours, vaine hope of inheritaunce, death by ouer ſtudy of his affaires & buſineſſe.

Luna, inheritaunce, riches by women, long life if ſhe be fortunate, ſhort life, impryſonment, ſlaunder by falſe witnes, ſtrife, ſuites, quarrells, & vexation of ſpirit, as madde or diſtraught of wittes.

The head of the Dragon, inheritaunce, riches, honor liberallitie, prodigallitie, and good death.

The tayle, horrible death, ſmall indeuour, no goodnes in the ſignification of this houſe.

In the ninth, Saturne betokeneth horrible dreames, terrible viſions, hypocriſie and ſuperſtition, ceremonies, preachers, Fryers, men of Religion, and a thouſande troubles, by the way and perturbation of ſpirit.

Iupiter, giueth faith, conſtancy in his religion, profitable iorneys, feare & loue of God, and knowledge of diuine miſteries, interpretations of dreames, reuelation and profit in the ſtate Eccleſiaſticall.

Mars, out of his princypall dignitie, daunger by the waye, vnfaythfulneſſe, ſhaking of the Fayth, and terrible Opinions and more then an Herytique, Timerous, Violent, Impudent: horrible Dreames, and falſe dexteritie in Armes and Valyantneſſe, when he is otherwiſe fortunate in his houſe or exaltation, it maketh the man very terrible, a Nigromancer, happy in his iorney or pilgrimages, hardy, ventrous, and of great courage.

Sol,

Sol, Benefices, Abbeyes, Bifhoprickes, Ecclefiafticall dignities, Cardinalls, Popes, Legates, principaly in a mafculine figne, good fayth, conftant, religious, a reuerencer of holy things, a louer of God and vertue, true dreames, profitable iorneys, and honor in his profeffion.

Venus, true dreames, except in the imagination of women, ecclefiafticall dignities, conftant Religion, loue and reuerence of God, long pilgrimage by the Worlde, profitable iorneys, honor in profeffion which taketh awaye the defire of marriage.

Mercurie, goodes Ecclesiafticall, high knowledge, diuine myfteries, admyration of iuftice and prouidence of God, cogitation of God & Angells, and of Spirits, profitable iorneys, great knowledge in diuinitie, Aftrologie, & in all other philofophie, interpretation of Dreames, Oracles, and ftraunge things, profit in trafique, in farre Countryes good renowne.

Luna, long pilgrimage, peruerfe cogitations, vnconftant in manners, and fortune, true dreames, knowledg of ftarres : When the ix. houfe is the houfe of Mercurie, or of other things anfwerable to the nature of the Lord of the ix. houfe.

The head of the Dragon, variable dreames, honour and profit in trauayle, Ecclesiafticall goods.

The tayle, lacke of Fayth, terrible Dreames, perillous iorneys, and full of enuie, and little honour in his profeffion.

In the tenth houfe, Saturne out of his principall dignities fignifieth fhort life of the mother, manye ill fortunes, Sighes, Playnts, & impryfonments. If the tenth houfe be in the figne of Leo, and any of the Lumynaries bee with Saturne, hee fhall die in pryfon. If Saturne be with Iupiter in the houfes of Iupiter, hee fhall be condempned of wronge : If hee be with Mars in the houfes of Mars, hee fhalbe condemned according to his crime. If hee be with Mercurie hee fhall dye a verye fhamefull death by falfe witneffes : If with Venus and Mars he fhalbe whipped &
racked

racked, & condemned to dye. Saturne in his houſe or exaltation in the tenth houſe, dooth licence dignities, preheminence, and gouernment.

Iupiter great honor in his profeſſion, ecclesiaſticall dignities, and great renowne.

Mars out of his principall dignities, maketh a man terrible, cruell, seditious, quarelſome, arrogant, a deſpiſer of his goodes, vſurper of the goodes of other, hated of Father, mother, bretheren, and other, and many tymes to be impryſoned and puniſhed by iuſtice. In his houſe or exaltation it maketh him valyant, hardie, couragious in feats of armes. In the houſes of Iupiter well diſpoſed, and regard of Fortunes, maketh him a Preſedent, Councellor, or ſoueraigne Iudge.

Sol giueth honour, offices, dignities, preheminences, rules, gouernments, great credit and fauour of many great Lords, in eſtimation of the common people, honour in profeſſion, with riches and great goodes, principally if he be in fierie Signes, and if the child be poore and of baſe condicion, hee lifteth him vp to honour and great dignities.

Venus honour in his profeſſion, goodes of Princes, and great Lordes, great credit, & long life of the mother, with proſperitie and honour.

Mercurie maketh him a Chauncellor, Secretary, Councellor, Preſident put in great dignities, skilfull in Arithmaticke, Geometrie, and, Aſtrologie well renowned, rich and abounding in goodes. If hee be vnfortunate by Mars, hee ſhall come to an euill ende, for hauing taken too much vppon him, or for taking quarrells againſt his betters.

Luna ſignifieth prayſe and honor of great Lordes, & ſhall be happy in all enterpriſes, and eſteemed in all the Worlde.

The head of the Dragon ſignifieth as Iupiter.

The tayle maketh him receiue diſhonour and loſſe of his calling, and falling from an highe, and denoteth the

ſhorte

shorte life of the Mother.

In the eleauenth house, Saturne out of his principall dignities betokneth acquaintance, and to be a companion with men defamed and of base condicion, mischieuous: sadnesse of friendes: vaine hope to come to things vndertaken: difficultie in affayres: losse of frindes, if hee bee in his house or exaltation, he giueth loue of Sarurnityes as by great & ancient Lords.

Iupiter maketh him happy in all his deuoyres: giueth fauour of great Lordes: great creditte: aboundaunce of friendes: aduancement by friendes: riches & fayre children: of the which the first shalbe a Maior.

Mars in his house or exaltation, loue by men of warre & fortunate in feats of armes, & out of those places signifieth dispayre, vnhappy enterprises, losse of friendes, & enmitie with his friends, he shall not be loyall to his lords & friendes: by which shall ensue great damage.

Sol, happy enterprises, goods, honor, dignities by meanes of friends which shalbe men of authority & great lordes.

Venus giueth good friends which shall bee honorable men: and of good authoritie: & of good will signifying good fortune: happy enterprises: & many children.

Mercurie knowledge: and company: & loue of men of knowledge and vertue: and good renowne amonge friends: happy enterprises.

Luna giueth good riches, honor, good renowne: good friends which shalbe great lordes: & happy enterprises.

The head of the Dragon, that which Iupiter signifieth.

The tayle, that which Saturne & Mars signifieth.

In the twelfth Saturne out of his principall dignities maketh vnhappye in Horses and other great Beastes, from the which hee shall fall and receaue hurte and signifieth feare of iustice, imprysonment or exile. In his House or Exaltation, victorye agaynst his enemies, good Fortune in Horses and other Beastes, fitte for burthen and labour.

Iupiter out of his principall dignities, mighty enemies
and

and Aduerſaries of men in authoritie, impryſonment, exile, condemnation, pouertie, well dignified hee ſignifieth
the contrary.

Mars the fall from Horſes, hurte or other damage by
beaſtes, aboundance of enemies, imprifonment, ſlaunders,
& a thouſand perſecutions, great euill in leggs & feete.

Sol, good fortune in Horſes and other great Beaſtes,
great perſecution by enemyes, greate Lordes, & mighty
confiſcation and loſſe of goodes, impryſonment, exile,
ſlaunder, falſe witnes, euill reporte, condemned to a great
fine, depriuation of his eſtate, by peruerted trayterous and
how ſhould ſeruants.

Venus, giueth good Fortune to Horſe, ſtrife and
enmytie to Women, diſprayſe in marriage, miſchieuous
and euill renowne becauſe of Women : principallye if
they bee euill condicioned and defamed, an impudent
Louer of Women defamed, for the which he ſhalbe impryſoned : and ſuffer great diſhonour. If ſhee be in the
ſigne of Virgo or Capricorne, or of Aquarius, ioyned with
the Sunne and Saturne, or to Mars ſignifieth great perill
of death by loue.

Mercurie giueth great knowledge, principally in ſcien-
ces that ſhall bring ſmall profit, maketh a man a philoſo-
pher, mathematician, & ready in al knowledge, a litle fooliſh by reaſon of the lightnes of the ſpirite, hauing manie
enemies, giuen to voluptuouſneſſe, euill fortune : hated by
men of knowledge, likely to be ſlaundered and impriſo-
ned. If Saturne be well diſpoſed he giueth good fortune
in horſes and other beaſtes.

Luna giueth many enemies which dayly ſhall grow &
increaſe, if ſhe be vnfortunate ſignifieth impriſonment &
exile, if ſhe be burnt & ioyned with Saturne or Mars, the
child ſhalbe euer miſerable and of a ſhort life, which ſhall
receiue hurt by beaſtes of like proportion : and dyeth by
plague, to be killed or drowned : If ſhee be fortunate it
betokeneth eſcape from all theſe euills.

The head of the Dragō betokeneth that which Iupiter.

　The

The tayle, damage by beaftes of like proportion and ruine by enemies.

And generally when a Planet is well dignified or otherwife well difpofed and regarded of fortunes within the fayd houfes, it fignifieth good lucke in all fignifications of the fayd houfes, but when it is vnfortunate, it yeeldeth mifchiefe in all the fayde fignifications.

CHAP. VIII.
The fignifications of the Lordes of the houfes by the places of the figure.

THE Lord of the firft houfe within the firft Fortune, betokneth long life, health of bodye, goodes, and riches by his owne proper meanes, honour of his parents. In the fecond, riches : In the third, often voiages, agreement and concorde with his bretheren. In the iiij. inheritaunces houfes and goodes vnmouable. And it noteth that he fhalbe a great builder, a planter of vines and trees, a medler with mines of golde and filuer, and other thinges according to the nature of the fayde planet : In the v. betokneth many children which hee fhall loue greatly, to be giuen to banquets, playes, dauncing, brauerie and to all voluptuoufnes and pleafure, and fhall haue many friendes to enrich him. In the vi. a buyer of fmall cattell, abounding in feruaunts the which he fhall teach and make dilligent, hee fhalbe fickly : In the feauenth, quarrelfome, giuen to ftrife and fuites in matters of marriage, vnfortunate in all his actes. In the viij. fadde, fearefull and of fhorte life. In the ix. an interpreter of Dreames, of Oracles, fecreate things and vifions, giuen to knowe diuine myfteries, to trauayle, and to abide in ftraunge Countreys. In the x. goodes, riches, dignities, and honor by the meanes of Princes and great Lords, good fortune in his profeffion. In the xi. happie enterprifes, good friendes, honourable companies, profperitie, fewe children. In the xii. euill manners, peruerfe nature; great enmitie, good fortune in cattell, If hee bee vnfortunate

nate in the firſt, the childe ſhall not liue long, if in the ſeconde, hee ſhall be deſtroyed and poore. If in the third,
he ſhall receiue great euill by his bretheren. If in the
fourth, he ſhalbe vnhappy in landes, inheritaunces, labor,
and poſſeſſions, and die in priſon. In the fifth, it denoteth
ſadneſſe and tribulation, be cauſe of children, & of meſſages and gifts, & ſhall many times die by too much drinke,
or by too much pleaſure. In the ſixth, ſignifieth great
ſicknes and piteous death. In the ſeauenth, by meanes
of the wiſe by poyſon, if he be in the ſigne of Capricorne,
by fire, if he be in a fierie ſigne, by fall from on high, if in
an earthly. In the eyght, ſhorte life, daunger of death in
trauayle. In the ninth, in perill to be ſlayne by theeues. In
the tenth, impriſonment, wracke, condemnation, & death
by meanes of princes. In the eleuenth, a thouſande euills,
and miſchiefes for friendes. In the twelfth, death in pryſon. The lord of the ſeconde in the firſt houſe ſignifieth
much gaine and to be rich; In the ſecond, that hee ſhall
haue much goodes and bee verye rich and auaricious.
In the third, loſſe by bretheren, & profit in ſmall voiages.
In the fourth, innumerable inheritaunces, augmentation
of patrimonie. In the fifth, profit in all things of pleaſure
and magnificence, children to come to honour, and ſhalbe
rich giuers. In the ſixth, profit by meanes of ſeruauntes,
and of keeping beaſtes In the ſeauenth, goodes of women, and by ſuites. In the eight, great downes: ſome inheritaunces, otherwiſe ſcattering of goodes. In the ninth,
goodes of the Church, fortunate in long pilgrimage. In
the tenth profit, profit in his profeſſion, goodes by greate
Lordes, and offices, and dignities. In the eleuenth, goods,
riches and honour by friendes. In the twelfth, profitte in
horſes and beaſtes, otherwiſe loſſe and iniuſtice by the
meanes of gayning. The lorde of the thirde houſe in the
firſt ſignifieth greater riches and prayſe then his bretheren, that he ſhall make many voyages. In the ſeconde, hee
ſhall haue ſuit with his bretheren for goodes. In third, he
ſhall often goe abroad for pleaſure, and his bretheren and

N   friendes

friends accompany him. In the iiii. he shall goe ofte to vi-
site his lands and posseffions, and his bretheren shall leaue
him, and with-holde parte of his right. In the v. his bretheren shall bee braue, pleasant, and gracious, and giuen
to voluptuousnesse, and make agreement with his Children. In the vi. that hee shall holde question of iniuries
with his bretheren and that they shall not answer him. In
the vii. suite against bretheren and friends, a voyage to be
married. In the viii. shorte life to bretheren flying for
feare of plague or murther. In the ix. pilgrimage of
friends, and voyages to obteyne pardons. In the x. voyages by reason of profeffion, and for dignities & death of
brethren and friendes. In the xi. good friendship among
brethren, voyages to meete with good fortune. In the xii.
enmities of bretheren, & voyages becaufe of enemies.

   The Lorde of the fourth in the first houfe, fignifieth
good difpofition and honour, richer then other of his
kyndred, a great man in buylding & poffeffions, and shall
builde houfes, plante vines, trees, and a diligent husband
in his grounds. In the fecond a good Traffiquer-in corne
Oyle, Wine, and Fruits, a deare feller and a good cheape
buyer, and a buyer and feller of Landes and Houfes. In
the thirde, hee shall haue the goodes and inheritaunce
of his Bretheren: in the fourth, hee shall haue greate
Fortune in goodes, Landes, Houfes and laboures, and
happen vppon Treafure. In the fifte, the riches of the
Father, Children happie in theyr inheritaunce. In the
fixt, fignifieth no great eftimation of the Father, but phificke, Surgerie and gouernment of ficke Folkes, and a
Nourifher of Beaftes: in the feauenth, inheritaunce by
Women, enmitie betweene the Father and Children, a
good hufwife of his wife: in the eight, the father of shorte
life, inheritaunce, death out of his Countrie: in the ninth,
lands, & poffeffions ioyned to the Church or in fubiectiõ
to the Church-men, and the father a ftraunger: in tenth,
the father to be knowne of great Lords, by the which shall
come greate profitte to the Childe, and shall haue lordships,

ſhips, Landes, and poſſeſſions by meanes of great Lords.
In the eleuenth, ſhorte life to the Father, inheritaunce by
friends: in the 12. the father a ſtranger & of baſe condiciō,
& ſhall hate his ſonne, & ſhall haue ſome mouable goods
of his enemies, not without long ſuite & great difficultie.

The Lorde of the fift, in the firſt houſe ſignifieth
feaſting, bankquetting, dauncing, voluptuouſnes, & faire
children. In the ſecond rich children & ioy of their gayning. In the third, voyages for pleaſure: in the iiii. goodes
of parents and alies: in the v. feaſtes, bankets, playes, brauerie, daunces, pleaſure and faire children: in the vi. witnes that he ſhalbe a peace-maker and not greatly giuen
to pleaſure: but in ſeruants & keeping cattell: in the vii.
the children ſhall hate the father, & ſhall haue ſuites one
againſt the other, yet alwayes contentment by his wife &
reioyce in her. In the viii ioyfull, becauſe of vnlooked for
inheritaunce, and ſhort life to children. In the ix. ioy in
pilgrimages, vowes, holy religion, good children that feare
and loue God. In the x. pleaſure in honour. In the xi.
pleaſure in freinds and many children. In the xii. ſhorte
life of children, enmitie betweene the father and the children, pleaſure in horſes.

The Lord of the ſixt in the firſt ſignifieth many ſickneſſes of the ſayd Lorde, and that his ſeruantes, and beaſtes
ſhall dye quickly. In the ſecond that he ſhall be rich by
keepinge of cattell. In the thirde, ſickneſſe and going
heere and there from home, a poore kindred. In the iiii.
that his Father ſhall bee of verye baſe condicion. In
the fith, Sickneſſe by ouer-much pleaſure, Children of
more baſe condicion then their father. In the vi. health
if the Lorde of the Aſcendant doe not regarde him, o-
therwiſe ſickneſſe by ouer-labour. In the ſeauenth, ſickneſſe by Women, of ſtrifes, and ſuites and ſtrife betweene
his ſeruauntes and him. In the eight, death by reaſon of
ſeruauntes. In the ninth, ſicke out of his Countrey by
trauayle. In the tenth, ſickneſſe by ouer-trauayle in
his Profeſſion, or by ouer-labouringe for honour.

In

In the xi. acquayntaunce of men vnknown, and ſickneſ by meanes of friends. In the xii. ſickneſſe by meanes of enemies and of impriſonment, and enemies of his owne Seruaunts.

The lorde of the vii. in the firſt ſignifieth gavne by traffique, peace and agreement, by exerciſe of phiſicke & Aſtrologie, and that he ſhalbe well loued of his wife, and haue goodes with her : but hee ſhalbe quarrelſome and haue ſuites. In the ii. ſhort life of his wife, ſuites for her goodes & riches : in the iij. ſtrife & ſuites againſt friends, kinsfolkes : and they ſhall loue his wife impudently. In the iiij. inheritaunce by women, ſuites againſt parents. In the v. a young Wife, honeſt and vertuous, beloued of her husband, and ſuite againſt his children. In the vi. ſtrife for cattell and ſeruaunts, marriage with ſome woman of baſe condition, or noted of ſome infamy proper to him-ſelfe and parents. In the vij. ſuits for women, houſholde-ſtrife, profit, and to agree and communicate his goodes. In the viij, ſtrife for inheritaunce, great goodes by women. In the ix. ſtrife and accuſations for matters of fayth, mar-riage with a ſtraunge woman : In the x. trouble for offi-ces and honour, an honourable wife, and dignitie by the wiues frindes. In the xi. ſuites againſt friends, or by their meanes, and ſhalbe married by his friends. In the xii. con-trouerſie againſt enemies, marriage with women of baſe condicion, and not long loue together.

The Lord of the eight in the firſt ſignifieth ire, ſadnes, angrie for that he cannot bring to paſſe, and ſhall not bee of long life. In the ii inheritaunce : in the iij. death of bretheren : in the iiij. death in his houſe, and ſhall ſee the death of his parents, and ſhall haue inheritaunces : in the v. death of children : in the vi. death of his familie before him, and ſhall be vnfortunate in cattell : in the vij. death of wife by whome he shall haue iuheritaunce, and thereby become rich : in the viij. that hee ſhall thinke ſodenly to die, and yet ſounde of bodie, trouble in ſpirite, and ſhall haue dower by his wife & inheritaunce, and other goods.

In

In the ix. that hee shall haue euill courage, and fhall dye out of his Countrie : in the x. honorable death, or other-therwife by the meanes of great Lordes, and of iudges, or becaufe of his honour : in the xi. death amongeft his friends : in the xii. death amongft his enemies, or by rea-fon of themfelues.

The Lord of the ninth in the firft fignifieth prudence, religious, vertuous, deuine, a louer of Church-men, and fhall make many voyages : in the ii. that hee shall make many voyages, by the which he shall become rich : in the iij. marriage out of his Countrie, or take a ftraunger, and shall make iourneys becaufe of his bretheren : in the iiii. death from home, pilgrimage by perfwafion of parents. In the v. haue childrĕ fiom home out of his Countrie & shall make iourneys for them : in the vi. marriage of a mayde or woman of bafe condicion, fickneffe from home, and fhall trauell for his feruauntes & cattell : In the vii. voyages and fuites by reafon of women and their goodes, and fignifieth the woman to be deuout, moderate, & well mānered : In the viii. defire of riches, trauell for his wiues goodes : In the ix. good vnderftanding, a louer of vertue, fearing God, knowledge in deuine myfteries, oracles, fe-crete thinges, and true dreames, trauell for deuotion : In the x. trauell for profeffion & honour : In the xi. good friendes from home : In the xii. euill courage, & enemies out of his Countrie, trauell by reafon of enemies.

The Lord of the tenth in the firft fignifieth that by his induftrie hee shall come to great honor, and shall haue dignitie, offices, and gouernments. In the fecond honour for his wealth : In the iii. honour by his bretheren, or by trauell : In the iiii. vnmouable goods, fumptuous houfes. In the v. honour by his children : In the vi. little honour, except of his houfhould and feruants, or in gouerning of the ficke. In the vii. honourable marriage : In the eight goodes by marriage, inheritaunce, and perill of death to the mother at the time of her trauell and delyuerie. In the ix. Ecclefiafticall dignitie, honour in ftraunge Countries,

　　　　　　　　　　　　　　　　　　　　　　　and

and eſtimation by his trauell. In the x. dignities, offices, and great honour by his owne meanes, and fauour of Princes. In the xi. proſperitie, honour, and fauour of friendes, In the xii. honour by his enemies, honour and eſtimation of men of euill condicion.

The Lord of the eleauenth, in the firſt ſignifieth good fortune, happy enterpriſes, good friends, and many children. In the ſecond, goodes, and riches by friends. In the third, amitie of bretheren, iorneys & trauayles for friends. In the fourth, good fortune in vnmouable goods. In the fift, aboundance of children, bankquets, ioy and good fortune. In the ſixte, fortune in good husbandrie. In the ſeauenth, rich and fortunate marriage, and good friendes, ſtrifes and debates againſt friendes, and that he ſhall bee poore in his youth, and rich in his age. In the eight, inheritaunce, death of friendes. In the ninth, profitable iorneyes, friendes out of his Countrye, and good fortune in ſtraunge places. In the tenth, goodes and honour by meanes of men of authoritie, and dignitie in youth. In the eleauenth, aboundance of friends, & children, great goods and honour, & fauour of men in authoritie, good renown and proſperitie. In the twelfth, ſmall friendes, few goods, and debate with his friends.

The Lord of the twelfth, in the firſt ſignifieth pouertie in youth, ſadneſſe, long trauell, enmytie and conſpiration againſt him. In the ſeconde euill manners, quarrells for goodes. In the third, quarrells with friendes and kyndred. In the fourth, ſtrife and ſuites for inheritaûnce and mouable goodes, and diſcorde with the father. In the fift, rebellious children to the father, and ſtrife amonge themſelues. In the ſixt, ſtrife and anger amonge the familie. In the ſeauenth, that hee ſhall take wiues of baſe condicion, ànd not loue them long, and by theyr meanes ſhall haue great paine and trauell, and ſhall bee in griefe for them, and his friendes ſhall conſpire againſt him, and his enemies ſhall take away part of his goodes, and in the ende of his dayes bee poore and miſerable. In the eight, hatred

hatred and treafon for lyuelyhood and goodes of women, death of enemies. In the ninth, quarrell with Church-men and mifchiefes by the way. In the tenth, quarrell with great Lordes, perfecution by reafon of his profeffi-on, of his offices and honour. The eleauenth, fignifieth that his friendes fhalbe his enemies, and fhall haue great mifchiefe for his friendes. In the twelfth, many enuies and enemies that fhall imagine many mifchiefes againft him.

Likewife, you muft iudge of all the partes of the xii. houfes, as the part of fortune in the firft fignifieth: that he fhalbe rich and fortunate by his induftrie. In the fecond, that he fhalbe come rich in all that is fignified by the fe-cond houfe, &c.

All thefe bee the foundations and rootes of the iudge-ments Aftronomical, from the which you may not fwarue or depart: Except in afmuch as be mittigated, prohiby-ted, or augmented by the Concurrences and afpeĉts of the Planets, and coniunĉion of the fixed ftarres.

The end of the fecond booke.

The third Booke of

Of Iudgementes Aſtronomycall vppon Natiuities, contayning the directions and reuolutions.

The third Booke.

Chap. I.
Of Directions.

THE art of Directions ſo dilygently entreated vpon by *Iohn de Regiomount*, that their is no more place fitly to ſpeake of the ſame. Except that with the ayde of God we haue purpoſed to tranſlate into French his problemes and documents appertayning to the ſayde matter. Neuertheleſſe we will here touch the the principall poynte. To direct (which tearme I vſe being being moſt commonly vſed and of long time receyued, although it bee not proper) it is no other thing then to ſtay the meeting of one place of the heauens with another conſequently following, acording to the naturall order of the ſignes, & that the mouing of the firſt mobile. The firſt place is named the ſignificator, the ſeconde the promittor: as if the aſcendant were in the xx. degree of Sagittarius & Saturne in the x of Capricorne, one might direct the aſcendant to Saturne & the aſcendant ſhallbee ſignificator of life, & Saturne promittor of death or ſickenes, & thē the iudgement ſhalbe danger of death, there is another form of direction attributed to the parts & planets retrogrades, which do make following the naturall courſe of the i. mobile, to the contrary of the conſequence of the ſignes, of the which the craft is like to the 1. & there is no

diffe-

difference but that wee haue called Significator, which is here promittor, and the Promittor is heere Significator.

The poynt meridionall of the tenth house, you muſt direct by the right aſcentions. The poynt of the aſcendant, by the aſcentions obliques, founde in the Table of the latitude of your Region. The poynts and ſtarres that ſhall be betweene the Merydian and the Horrizon, by the oblique aſcentions vnder the circle in the which they be, the which you call, The cyrcle of Poſition, the which for to finde, and likewiſe to haue the aſcentions of euery place hauing latitude or no, you muſt follow the methode following.

Firſt, you muſt take the longitudes of Plannets, fixed ſtarres, and other places that you would direct (that is to ſay) the ſigne, degree, and mynute that they holde in the Zodiack and in the Ephemerides, or other tables Aſtronomicall. &c.

Secondly, you muſt calculate their latitudes, in degrees and mynutes placed in the Ephemerides.

Thirdly, theyr declination by the firſt probleame of the booke of directions of Regiomont.

Then, theyr right aſcentions by the third probleame of the ſayde houſe.

Then againe, the diſtances of the circle Meridional by the nineteenth probleame.

Incontinent, the circles of their poſitions, by the twentith probleame, conſequently the dyfferences aſcentional by the Table expreſſed.

And finally the oblique aſcentions by the tenth Canon, if the ſayd ſtarres be betweene the poynt meridionall of the tenth houſe, and the poynt of the fourth, or the diſcentions of obliques by the eleuenth probleame, if they be betweene the poynt of the fourth and the tenth.

Thys done, take out the number of the oblique aſcentions of the Significator, of the number of the oblique aſcentions of the Promittor, take to the Table of the poſition of the Significator, or the centrary, if you direct the parts and Planets retrogrades; that which refteth of degrees & minutes, turne into yeres, monthes & dayes: and by this meanes, you fhall haue exactly the time of good or euill that fhall happen vnto you by direction, intending that one degree is heere fignified a yeere, fiue mynutes a month, one minute 6. dayes & fome od howers, he that would helpe the feconds hee fhall touch the ende more perfectly.

For to know the ficknefles and daunger of death, you muft direct the fiue vital places that we haue confidered, fearching the gyuer of lyfe, in fixed ftarres of violent nature in the poynt of the fourth, fixt, feauenth and eyght, and the tayle of the Dragon, to the ill fortunes and theyr euill afpects in the partes of death, and by and by to the Sunne, and to the head of the Dragon. Likewife for the fame confideration, you muft direct the faide pernicious places to the fiue vitall places. And they meeting, they iudge that the man is in great danger of death, when the Fortunes doe not fhewe foorth theyr fauourable beames.

For the goods, honour, dignities, friendfhips, and other confiderations, you muft direct the one fignificator of goods with the other, and the one fignificator of honour with the others, of the which wee haue made mention in the firft Booke, following the particuler iudgements of the natiuities.

Chap. II

Of the Seperator or Burner, called of the
Arabians, Algebuthar.

THE Seperator or Burner, is the Planet which hath dignitie of tearme & degree, to the which the yeere is aunfwerable, mutiplied with the afcentions of one Significator.

For to finde the Seperator of the like, you muft take the Oblique afcentions of the afcendant, and adde vnto the fame the yeeres of your age, and fearch it all in the
Table

Table of the latitude of your Region, to looke to which
figne and degree the faide number aunfwereth, for vnto
that poynt fhall come the perfection of your life. Looke
afterwarde which is the Plannet which hath dignitie of
tearme in the faid degree, for of the felfe fame fhall be the
Seperator of the life.

By the fame meanes you may feeke the Seperators of
the honour, goods, gaynes, friendes, and of other lyke,
vpon the circles of theyr pofitions. The which is conuenient to feeke following the afore-faid methode of directions.

CHAP. III.
Of the Lords of the Triplicities.

YOV muſt alfo note all the Lordes of the Triplicities, in places which fignifie good and euill, as well
in fignifications of lyfe, as of goods, friendes, honor,
marriages, pylgrimages.&c. If they be wel difpofed
in the reuolution, they fhall fignifie well, touching the
fignification of the place of the which they be Lordes. If
they be vnfortunate, they fignifie euill. That is to vnder-
ftand, the Lords of the tryplicities of vitall places, wil fignifie of the life: of the places of fortune, riches & profit:
of places of honour, of the honour, good or euill, according as they be fortunate or vnfortunate at the hower, of
the reuolution.

CHAP. IIII.

Of Reuolutions.

THE Sunne returning to the fame poynt in the
which he was at the hower of the natiuity, maketh
the reuolution euery yeere. He therfore that wold
know the hower and mynute of the reuolution, he
muſt looke in the Ephemerides, at what hower and mynute the Sunne beganne to enter into the degree minute
and fecond, in which he was at the hower of the natiuity.

If

If the Ephemerides doe not fuffife you for thys matter, goe to a Table made for the fame purpofe, by *Peter Pitat*, in the beginning of the fame Ephemerides, by him correcſted and augmented. *Ierom Cardin* vfeth another, which I finde very exaſt: the which hee hath written in his booke, Of the reſtitution of times and celeſtiall motions, in the fyſt Chapter.

CHAP. V.
Of the iudgements vpon the reuolutions.

Irſt looke howe the Seperator of lyfe is difpofed in the figure of the reuolution: for if hee be vnfortunate, he denoteth ficknes and other daungerous accidents ; If he be fortunate, he holdeth him healthfull and glad all the yeere. So likewife you muſt iudge of the Seperator of goods, friends, dignities & other effeſts. It is to vnderſtand, that they giue good fortune in the faid fignifications, if they be well difpofed : or els loſſe & euill fortune if they be vnfortunate.

In the fecond place, looke if the Lords of the Tryplicities of the vitall places be well difpofed: and of places which fignifie riches, honour, trauailes, bretheren, Parents, wiues and children, doe fo much. For in the fame fignifications the man fhall be happy or vnhappy, according as the fayd Lords fhall be wel or euil difpofed. And principally you muſt confider the Lord that fhall raigne ouer your age : for the firſt Lord of one tryplicity gouerneth the firſt age ; the fecond, the middeſt of the life ; the third, the latter yeere.

Thirdly, you muſt confider which is the Planet which gouerneth ouer the yeere of your age, that which the *Arabians* call *Fridaie*.

Fourthly, the Lorde of the Signe in which fhall come the fame yeere of perfeſtion.

In the fiſt place, the Lord of the circulation, accounting by the Lord of the houre of the natiuity.

Then the Lord of the circulation, accounting by the
Lord

Lord of the afcendant of the natiuitie.

And if in the afcendant of the natiuitie there be anie Planet, you muft likewife make circulation.

Furthermore, you muft looke if any Planet returne to the fame figne and houfe, in the which it was at the natiuitie; for then it intendeth the fame effect which it hath fignifyed in the natiuity, principally when it returneth to the fame figne. You muft alfo haue regard to the afpects which are made in the reuolution, if they be like to them of the natiuity: for that fhal be a renuing of the effects of the faid afpects.

And you muft not forget the chaunging of the places. For if a happy Plannet bee in the reuolution in the place where an euill Planet was in the natiuity, the euill fignified by the fayd euill Planet in the natiuitie, fhall be deferred that yeere by the prefence of the happy Planet. To the contrary, if a Planet promife any good fortune in the natiuitie, and in hys place in the reuolution be any vnfortunate Planet, the fame good fignifyed in the natiuitie, fhalbe diminifhed in the reuolutiõ, or loft by reafon of the faid ill fortune. The mif-fortune in the places of mif-fortune augmenteth the euill, the good fortunes in the places of good fortune, augmenteth the good fortune.

For to iudge of the faid confiderations, you muft haue recourfe to that which we haue fayde in the two former Bookes of generall and particuler fignifications of the Houfes, Signes, Planets, afpects, & particuler fituations of the Planets in fignes and houfes: hauing alwaies before your eyes, the difpofition of ftarres in the figure of the natiuitie. For if a Planet be in the natiuity greatly vnfortunate, and in the reuolution well difpofed, it cannot much profite becaufe of the firft infelicity.

Likewife you muft iudge of thofe which bee fortunate in natiuities, which being vnfortunate in reuolucions, do no great damage. There be fome that contemplate herevpon, many other things, the which by experience I haue often found vnprofitable, falfe, and fuperfluous.

Chap.

Chap. VI.
Of the yeeres gouerned by the Planets, called of the Arabians Fridarie.

IF the natiuite be by day, then the Sunne gouerneth the fyrſt tenne yeeres, Venus eyght yeres following, Mercurie thirteene yeeres after that : then the Moone, the nine following. Saturne eleuen yeeres, Iupiter twelue, Mars feauen, the head of the Dragon three, the tayle of the Dragon two. When it is by night, you muſt beginne at the Moone, the which gouerneth the firſt nine yeeres, then Saturne, Iupiter, Mars, Sol, Venus, Mercurie, the head of the Dragon, and the tayle, the numbers by order as we haue fayd before.

Many by great curiofitie, haue added to this companie other Planets to euery gouernment, the which I finde by good reaſon to be reprehended by the Chaldeans. For experience hath often taught mee and other very expert in this Science, that this ſubtiltie is too curious, vaine and ſuperfluous.

The

The Table of the *Fridaries* by Daie.

	Yeeres.	Monthes.	Dayes.
☉	1	5	5
☉☉☿	2	10	9
☉☉ 4	4	3	13
☉☉ D	5	8	17
☉☉ ♄	7	2	21
☉☉ 4	8	6	26
☉☉ ♂	10	0	0
☿	11	1	22
☿ ☿	12	3	13
☿ D	13	5	4
☿ ♄	14	6	26
☿ 4	15	8	17
☿ ♂	16	10	9
☿ ☉	18	0	0
☿	19	10	9
D	21	8	17
♄	23	6	2
4	25	5	14
♂	27	3	13
☉	29	1	22
☿	30	0	0
D	32	3	13
D ♄	33	6	26
D 4	34	10	9
D ♂	36	1	22
D ☉	37	5	5
D ☿	38	8	17
D ☿	40	0	0

	Yeeres.	Monethes.	Dayes
♄	41	6	26
♄ 4	43	1	22
♄ ♂	44	8	18
♄ ☉	46	3	14
♄ ☿	47	10	10
♄ ☿	49	5	6
♄ D	50	0	0
4	52	8	17
4 ♂	54	5	4
4 ☉	56	1	21
4 ☿	57	10	8
4 ☿	59	6	26
4 D	61	1	22
4 ♄	63	0	0
♂	64	0	0
♂ ☉	65	0	0
♂ ☿	66	0	0
♂ ☿	67	0	0
♂ D	68	0	0
♂ ♄	69	0	0
♂ 4	70	0	0
♌	73	0	0
☋	75	0	0

The

The Table of the *Fridaries* by Night.

	Yeeres	Monthes	Dayes		Yeeres	Monethes	Dayes
☽	1	3	13	☉	40	5	50
☽ ♄	2	6	26	☉ ♀	42	10	10
☽ ♃	3	10	9	☉ ☿	43	3	15
☽ ♂	5	1	22	☉ ☽	44	8	20
☽ ☉	6	5	5	☉ ♄	46	1	25
☽ ♀	7	8	18	☉ ♃	47	7	0
☽ ☿	9	0	0	☉ ♂	49	0	0
♄	10	6	26	♀	50	1	2
♄ ♃	12	1	22	♀ ☿	51	3	13
♄ ♂	13	8	18	♀ ☽	52	5	6
♄ ☉	15	3	14	♀ ♄	53	6	26
♄ ♀	16	10	9	♀ ♃	54	8	20
♄ ☿	18	5	6	♀ ♂	55	10	8
♄ ☽	20	0	0	♀ ☉	57	0	0
♃	21	8	17	☿	58	10	9
♃ ♂	23	5	4	☿ ☽	60	8	17
♃ ☉	25	1	21	☿ ♄	62	6	26
♃ ♀	26	10	8	☿ ♃	64	5	4
♃ ☿	28	6	25	☿ ♂	66	3	13
♃ ☽	30	3	13	☿ ☉	68	1	21
♃ ♄	32	0	0	☿ ♀	70	0	0
♂	33	0	0	☊	73	0	0
♂ ☉	34	0	0	☋	75	c	0
♂ ♀	35	0	0	☽	76	3	13
♂ ☿	36	0	0	☽ ♄	77	6	26
♂ ☽	37	0	0	☽ ♃	78	10	9
♂ ♄	38	0	0	☽ ♂	80	1	22
♂ ♃	39	0	0	☽ ☉	81	5	5

Chap.

Chap. VII.

Of profectinos.

FOR the profections you muſt reſolue the twelue
houſes of your natiuity in equall partes vppon the
Eclipſe, ſo farre as the aſcendant is in the firſt degree
of any Signe: the ſeconde houſe ſhall be in the fyrſt
degree of a ſigne following, and the thirde, in the firſt degree of a thirde ſigne: and to conclude, that euery houſe
beginne by the fyrſt degree, as the firſt houſe.

Alſo, euery houſe will containe thirtie degrees, & the
firſt thirty degrees of the firſt houſe, ſhall appertaine to
the fyrſt yeere wherein the infant is borne; the thirtie of
the ſecond, to the ſecond yeere: the thirty of the thirde to
the third yeere, & ſo conſequently vntill twelue. Twelue
yeeres paſſed, you muſt begin againe at the firſt, and then
come to the ſecond, third, fourth &c. and ſo from twelue
to twelue you muſt renue the ſame circuite.

If you finde the reuolution within the thirtie degrees
ſeruing to your yeere, it ſignifieth ſome good or euil, according to his nature or good or euill diſpoſition, & ſignification of the place, of which ſhall be the ſayd profection; that is to ſay, of the places of lyfe, ſicknes, death, or
good health; of the places of goods, riches, loſſe, or pouertie. &c. Commonly they ſeeke the profection of fyue
places of one natiuitie, that is to ſay, of the place of the
Sunne for honour; of the place of the Moone for the
qualities of the ſpyrit, towardes the body and externall
goods; of the place of the parte of Fortune, for gaine and
profite; of the tenth houſe for the actions; of the aſcendant for the lyfe.

If the Sunne be gyuer of lyfe, it muſt be conſidered as
gyuer of lyfe and giuer of honor likewiſe, the which you
muſt doe alſo in other places, when they import manie
ſignifications. If then you finde any Plannet within the
thirtie degrees of your profection, and would know what

moneth or day the accident by him signifyed shal happen.

Looke what distance you haue betweene the first point of your profection, and the said Plannet, if there be xv. degrees betweene them, the saide accident shall happen out in the ende of sixe moneths: if it be twentie-fiue degrees, at the end of tenne monethes: for heere two degrees and a halfe, value one moneth; one degree valueth twelue dayes and foure houres, thirty minutes value sixe daies, fiue minutes one day.

Of this there is a verie exact table among the documents of *Peter Ryss* vpon the Ephemerides: Example of the profections. Suppose that the ascendant of a natiuitie was the fifteene degree of Scorpius, I would know where the profection shal light of the ascendant at the ende of tenne yeeres after the childborne. I accoun tenne signes from the ascendant, after that, I finde the fifteene degree of Virgo seruing after tenne yeeres, accomplished to xj. currant. I say then that in the said time, the profection of the ascendant is come in the fifteene degree of Virgo, & shall end that yeere in the fifteene degree of Libra: and also shal containe thirty whole degrees, within the which if any Planet be founde, it shall signifie good or guill of the life, according to the nature & disposition as if in the said time.

Mars being in the fifo degree of Libra, I woulde say that the infant should be troubled that yeere at the end of eyght monethes, because that Mars was in the place profectionall of life, distant from the first poynt twentie degrees. We haue shewed before, that two degrees and a halfe value one month, fiue degrees two monthes, and fifteene degrees sixe monthes, and by course twenty degrees eyght monethes. You must note, that the profections ought to fitte to the yeeres currant or complete. It is to be vnderstoode the tenth signe, as for incontinent after nine yeeres complete, which is tenne yeeres currant.&c.

CHAP. VIII.
The Lords of the circulations from the howers of the Natiuities.

THE Babilonians hold for a great secrete, the Circulation of the Lord of the hower of the natiuitie? It is to be vnderstood, that the Lord of the said houre signifieth of the life as the ascendant, and the Lord of the hower following, of goods as of the second house : and the Lord of the third hower, of bretheren as the third house, and so consequently of others.

In Reuolutions, they giue the Lorde of the hower of the natiuitie to the first yeere, the Plannet following to the second, and so consequently following the natural order of the Planets. As if one were borne in the hower of Venus, that Planet should raigne the first yeere, the second yeere, Mercurie, the third, the Moone, the fourth, Saturne, the fift, Iupiter, the sixt, Mars, the seauenth Sol, the eyght, Venus, the ninth, Mercurie, and so by order. And you must note, that wee take heere the yeeres currant, and not complete, for to fit the sayde circulation of the Planets.

CHAP. IX.
Of the circulation of the Lord of the Ascendant, and the Planets which are in the Ascendant.

THE circulation of the Lord of the Ascendant, and the Planets and parts which be in the Ascendant, they be euen as we haue saide of the Lorde of the houre of the natiuitie, and by the same order you must place them. The yeeres of the age of the Chyld, by iudgement, we haue made mention and proofe of Reuolutions.

Chap.

Chap. X.

*Of Eclipses and great coniunctions appertaining
to Reuolutions of Natiuities.*

THE Eclipse of the Sunne, and the coniunction of
the Superiour Planets, causeth commonly many e-
uils, after the congruence of the starres, and nature
of the signes and Plannets raigning in the saide places, to men causeth sicknesses, when they be within the
fiue next degrees of the Ascendant, or to the gyuer of
lyfe: if they touch the other parts, Plannets or houses,
they pronounce euill fortune, appertaining to the significations of the same places; princlpally, if in the same time
of the natiuitie, any such constellations were in force. If
they touch the places perfectionals, they doe almost the
same effect as in natiuities.

Chap. XI.

*Of the particuler meetings of the whole
yeere.*

COncerning the particuler meetings of all the yere,
Ptolomeus, Iohn de Regiomonte, Ganrique, and manie others, doe rest harde vppon the Profections,
Mensturnes and Diurnes, of the which you haue
a perfect Table in the Booke of Directions of *Iohn de Regiomonte,* hauing more subtiltie & curiousnes then trueth,
as I haue often found by experience. It aunswereth better my opinion *Schonor,* which euerie day considered, if
any Planet touch the places of the Planets, parts & houses, of the natiuitie or their good or euill aspect, that I doe
apply to the places profectionall. As for example, let the
ascendant of a natiuitie, or the place of his profection bee
the twelfe degree of Libra, the Sunne in the fifteenth of
Geminy, Mars in the fifteenth of Leo: alwaies, and as often as the Sunne or the Moone doe passe ouer the xv.
degree of Leo, the man shall bee mooued by angry acci-
dentes, as of displeasure, of some alteration, payne of the
head,

head, Feauer, hote Impoftumes, Tetters.&c. Likewife
when it toucheth the fyft degree of Scorpius, or of Taurus, there where the quadrate afpects be within the place
of Mars, or the fift of Aquarius, which is the place oppo-
fite to Mars. If any Planet touch the fift degree of Libra,
or of Gemini (there where the Sextile afpects be) or the
fift of Sagitarius and of Aries, (which make the Tryne
afpects of the faide Mars) it fhall fignifie fome fauourable meetings of Captaines and men of warre.

If the ill fortunes touch not the faide twelfe degree of
Libra, as we haue faid in the Afcendant, that fhalbe figne
of fome euill meeting, as well to life as to the body. Likewife you muft iudge of other attouchments, according to
the nature of the afpects, by vs explained in the feconde
Booke. You muft contemplate the places profectionals.
For I doe apply euerie degree and minute to the dayes in
the which their fignification fall, and regard the good &
euill afpects of the Planets euery day, if they touch the
degree profectionall. As for example, of the faid natiuitie in the which was the Afcendant Libra, fuppofe that
the profection was come to the twelfe degree of Cancer,
in the ninth yeere complete and the tenth currant. The
thirteenth degree of Cancer, ferueth to the twelfe day after the proper day of the reuolution.

Wherefore I confider then the afpects of the Planets
towards the faide thirteenth degree. Likewife fo I do of
other degrees and minutes, fitted to thofe daies in the
which they gouerne. And fo much for Reuolutions.

FINIS.

P 3.

www.ingramcontent.com/pod-product-compliance
Lightning Source LLC
Chambersburg PA
CBHW020251290526
45784CB00003B/1198